ANCIENT ITALY

AND

MODERN RELIGION

T0382336

ANCIENT ITALY AND MODERN RELIGION

BEING THE
HIBBERT LECTURES FOR 1932

BY

ROBERT SEYMOUR CONWAY

Litt.D. (Cantab., Manc.); Hon. Litt.D. (Dub.); Hon. D.Litt. (Oxon.); Dott. on. Univ. (Padua);
Fellow of the British Academy; Hon. Fellow of Gonville and Caius College, Cambridge; some time
Professor of Latin in University College, Cardiff, and recently in the University of Manchester; Knight
Commander of the Order of the Crown of Italy; Corresponding Member of the German Archaeological
Institute; and of the American Academy of Arts and Sciences; Author of The Italic Dialects,
Harvard Lectures on the Vergilian Age, Makers of Europe; *joint*
Editor of Livy i–v, vi–x, xxi–xxv.

CAMBRIDGE
AT THE UNIVERSITY PRESS
MCMXXXIII

CAMBRIDGE UNIVERSITY PRESS
Cambridge, New York, Melbourne, Madrid, Cape Town,
Singapore, São Paulo, Delhi, Mexico City

Cambridge University Press
The Edinburgh Building, Cambridge CB2 8RU, UK

Published in the United States of America by Cambridge University Press, New York

www.cambridge.org
Information on this title: www.cambridge.org/9781107623453

First published 1933
First paperback edition 2013

A catalogue record for this publication is available from the British Library

ISBN 978-1-107-62345-3 Paperback

ANDREAE GEORGIO LITTLE

indefessae XL annorum amicitiae

memor

PREFACE

IN accepting the invitation with which I was honoured by the Hibbert Trustees to be their lecturer for 1932, remembering that the theme of the lectures as defined by the Will of the Founder may be "any subject bearing upon the history of Christianity", I ventured to make one assumption. It cannot, I feel sure, be desirable that each lecturer in turn should make some new attempt to set forth in his brief course his own particular conception of the more general aspects of religious history or religious philosophy. The purpose of the foundation can be better served, in the case of one whose work has run in well-marked lines, if he tries to acquaint his hearers or readers with one or two particular sides of the study that he has been pursuing which seem to him to throw light upon the history of religious ideas. He may be well content if the facts which he describes can suggest some new points of view from which to examine our modern problems.

It follows that not a little of the subject-matter of this volume will be known, if not familiar, to a certain number of my old pupils at Cardiff and Manchester, and to the audiences at the lectures I have given in what has become almost an annual visit to the John Rylands Library. Nevertheless, all these lectures were written for a place in a course of this kind, save that the fifth was re-written from this standpoint, on the basis of an interpretation of Vergil's story of Dido which I have maintained for over thirty years, and which I believe was first printed in an address to the Classical Association of Scotland in 1913. The fourth and the sixth were delivered as part of a special course of lectures on Vergil given in the University College of Wales, Aberystwyth, in October, 1931, and I am grateful to the liberality of the College regulations which allow me to publish them in this volume. The second and third lectures were first delivered in the John Rylands Library and I have to thank the Librarian, Dr Henry Guppy, for his kindness, which is now well-known, in permitting me to re-publish them in a form only slightly modified from that in which they were printed in the John Rylands Library Bulletin.

The text of the lectures, as here presented, has been freed from a great number of faults, both in form and in substance, by the vigilant scrutiny of my friend Mr Ernest Harrison, of Trinity College, now Registrary of the University of Cambridge, who generously found time to read through the whole proof, and to whom I owe cordial thanks. I have also to thank one or two other friends for assistance of different kinds which is acknowledged at the relevant points. For some of the illustrations I have further to thank Mr H. M. Bower, and the Folk-Lore Society; the Council of the Society for Hellenic Studies; the Clarendon Press as Publishers of Dr Randall-MacIver's *The Etruscans*, and Sir Arthur Evans, Bt., for kindly allowing me to reproduce illustrations which were their property. The pictures of the Venetic goddess Rehtia and her ritual are borrowed from my own contribution (namely the part relating to Venetic) to the *Records of the Prae-Italic Dialects of Italy*, by Professor J. Whatmough, Mrs Sarah Elizabeth Johnson and myself, which will be published in three volumes by the Clarendon Press, shortly before or after the appearance of these lectures.

Since the study on which these lectures are based, and which has extended over several years, has been mainly carried out in the Library of the British Museum, I may be allowed the pleasure of expressing my gratitude to Mr Arthur J. Ellis, the Superintendent of the Reading Room, and his colleagues Messrs G. F. Rendall and H. Sellers, for the untiring kindness of their friendly and always effective help.

For kind advice as to form and style of printing I have to thank Mr S. C. Roberts, Secretary to the Syndics of the Cambridge University Press and Mr W. Lewis, Printer to the University. Last, but not least, the book is throughout indebted to the thoughtful skill of my secretary, Miss Ruth Walker, and the Index of Names is almost wholly her work.

R. S. C.

St Albans
June 1933

CONTENTS

ILLUSTRATIONS

CHAPTER I

PICTURES OF PRE-ROMAN RELIGION

IN the course of many years' study of Ancient Italy, directed mainly upon linguistic and literary lines, it has happened to me to become familiar with some of the features of the religion of the Italian peoples outside Rome which are little known as compared with the half-Greek mythology that was current in Rome itself in the last century B.C. These features have nevertheless, as I hope to make clear, contributed something to the common stock of ideas which Europe took over in or with the Christianity which it drew from Rome. And in another part of my duties it has been natural to me in reading again and again the great Roman writers that immediately preceded the Christian era, especially the poet Vergil, to observe with interest some aspects of their ethical and religious attitude which have contributed more than a little to shaping the new faith. The first half of this book, therefore, will be given to certain non-Roman religious practices in different parts of Italy; and the latter half to the final struggle, so to speak, of paganism with itself, or perhaps, more truly, the struggle of the beams of light from Greek thought, travelling through Roman channels, with the grossnesses and opacities of primitive Italian belief. We shall find, if I mistake not, that this struggle is by no means over yet; and that the efforts to which thinking men of all nations are urgently summoned by the present appalling needs and troubles of human society as a whole may be at least clarified, if not actually aided, by observing how needs and troubles not wholly dissimilar were regarded by the greatest writers of that older day.

In one thing, ancient religion certainly differs markedly from religion as we know it in post-Puritan England, I mean its lighter aspects. The human animal can be playful and amusing as well as tragic, and the religions of Italy, both past and present, cannot be well understood if they are always regarded *au grand sérieux*.

In this first essay I will try to show, by word and picture, some of the things that have been recently ascertained about the cults of certain deities whom in a sense one may call local. One set come from the ancient Umbrian city now called Gubbio; and the other from the Venetic city now called Este which was one of the seats of the thoughtful and artistic race from which the culture of Venice ultimately sprang. The religious habits of these two races made different contributions to our modern stock of ideas; but in some respects both are typical of Italian religion.

One of the most ancient monuments in Italy is the famous Iguvine[1] Tables; they are of bronze, and seven of them are still preserved in the Town Hall of Gubbio; two are said to have been 'lost' long ago. These Tables are engraved with documents containing different parts of the Liturgy of a certain priestly brotherhood, and they give directions for the performance of different rites;

[1] By some mediaeval blunder, possibly a misreading of the Tables themselves, the name 'Eugubine' was long in use; but it has no ancient authority whatever. The name of the city was Iguvium and its ethnic adjective, both in Latin and Umbrian, was *Iguvinam* (if I may take a form in which the case ending is the same in both dialects, Latin and Umbrian).

one of these parts, in point of elaboration the longest and therefore probably the most important, concerns a procession made from one point to another round the town, especially to the different gates, at each of which victims were sacrificed and prayers said; some of these we will consider presently. Five of the Tables, or strictly four and two-thirds, are engraved in the local Iguvine alphabet which is derived from the Etruscan alphabet; but the last two Tables and the last third of one other, though still written in the Umbrian dialect, are engraved in Latin alphabet, and these last two Tables show a later stage[1] of the language. The oldest of these seven tablets seems from its alphabet to have been engraved between 400 and 300 B.C. and the latest about 80 B.C., one of the results of the Social War in 90–89 B.C. having been the universal adoption for any public purpose of the Latin alphabet throughout Italy, except in the Greek cities.

The directions given in this liturgy for the promenade round the town have come down to us in two editions. One, the older form,[2] is written in the local alphabet; the other, which is the later form, is written still in the Umbrian dialect, with changes like that just mentioned, but in the Latin alphabet of about 90 B.C. In the older edition the officer who performs the rite is instructed to 'pray silently'. What he is to pray is for the most part left to his own memory or discretion; but in the later form, although he is still ordered to 'pray without speaking', which means presumably 'in a whisper', the com-

---

[1] For example, 'before the gates' in the older Tables is *pre veris*, but in the later *pre verir*.

[2] Table IA; the later version in Table VIA.

piler of the liturgy thinks it best to provide him with
the actual words that he is to use.

There seem to have been about five stages in the performance at each of the gates or other halting-places.
First of all the 'officer with the herald's staff', the beadle
as we should call him, solemnly proclaims that all who
belong to any one of four tribes, of whom the Etruscans
are one, all four being presumably more or less hostile
to the city, are warned to depart. If they don't depart,
anyone who catches them hiding is instructed to 'carry
them where they ought to be carried, and do with them
what ought to be done', a cryptic formula which is
generally understood to mean something sufficiently dis-
agreeable, throwing them over a cliff, or the like. The
notice has to be repeated three times. When these un-
friendly bans have been duly proclaimed, the citizens of
Iguvium themselves are told to 'make themselves holy
and gather together in their proper divisions'. Then the
officiating priests proceed, with various chosen persons
of an inferior degree of sanctity, apparently appointed for
the occasion (*praenovatos*), first of all to take the omens.
Appropriate prayers are followed by a holy silence while
they watch for the proper birds, who have to appear, if
they are sufficiently gracious, and of the quite proper and
legitimate breeds, namely a woodpecker and a crow and
a pair of jays, within the proper augural lines in the sky,
drawn by imagination over certain portions of the city.

When these omens have been duly obtained, the priests
proceed with the sacrifices at three different gates, at
each of which particular victims are prescribed, oxen or
pigs or heifers or sheep or bull calves, always three in
number. In each case some wine or vinegar is poured

out and very long prayers are said, addressed to a different
deity (or deities) at each place over each victim; but all
of them to the same effect, invoking blessings upon
various classes of the people and various parts of the city.
Much the same kind of thing happens at two temples, and
this completes the purification of the Citadel.

The lustration[1] of the people is a longer business, at
least the prayers are even longer; they are not delivered
at temples, but at more picturesque places, such as 'the
Fountains' and 'the Blackberry Bush' (though we are not
to interpret the names as being houses of public refreshment, only as turning points in the topography of the
city). There are points of interest in the prayer, which
is the same in all the places, though addressed sometimes to all three and sometimes to only one of three
deities, namely, Cerfus Martius, who is masculine, and
two feminine deities who belong to him, one called
Praestita and the other called Tursa.[2] Whether they are
wives or daughters or merely sacred attendants does not
appear. It is clear that the business of Tursa, the third
of the group, is to frighten people, though she can be
kind if she chooses. Probably the duty of Praestita is
just the reverse, to provide help or food, though she can
refuse it if she chooses. We shall perhaps find more light
on these deities later on. The most striking thing in all
three prayers is the greater fulness with which evil is
invoked upon the four enemy tribes than are the blessings
upon the people of Iguvium. The latter are briefly included in the phrase 'be kind and bless them with peace',

[1] Table IB and IIA (first half); the later version is in VIB and VIIA.
[2] It is convenient to use these names in the form they would have had
in Latin.

though the different classes of citizens, noblemen belted and not belted, whoever they were, men of war with spears and without, are fully enumerated; but the curse is tremendous. ' Make them fear and make them tremble. Throw them down and trip them up. Snow upon them, rain upon them. Thunder at them, smite them. Lame them and bind them in fetters.' And the curse, be it observed, comes first. That was the real thing. When their enemies had been thus properly dealt with, the blessings desirable for the people themselves might be enumerated in few words. It is curious how the gods of primitive peoples are instructed with much more fulness to do harm than to do good; but all that concerns our own enquiry is to note that the conception of a deity who was glad to do good for its own sake was remote from the Italian peasant.

Yet we have evidence that the good people of Iguvium, although they wished their enemies properly cursed, found many other cheerful occupations for this presumably annual festival. In some of the regulations[1] of the Brotherhood we read of a banquet accompanied by sacred (but no doubt very cheerful) 'jumpings', and of a vote being taken at the end to say whether the brethren have been satisfied with the way the whole festival has been conducted and if not, how heavy a fine is to be inflicted on the steward. Other regulations state the quantity of corn and the number of beasts which the brethren are to receive from various estates.

One of the earliest of the documents[2] which the Tables contain gives directions for the conduct of a ceremony, which includes a procession, on a fixed day of every year,

[1] Table V.   [2] Tables III and IV.

which there is some reason[1] for thinking may have been at the opening of the month of May, though the meaning is not quite certain. It may or may not have been part of the lustration just described. But it has one curious feature; the sheep who is to be ultimately sacrificed is carried about in some kind of cage, which appears to be elevated upon a stretcher; and when he finally reaches the field in which the sacrifice is to take place, apparently a framework of two storeys was erected beside or under or perhaps more probably on the top of the cage, and each storey had to be carefully marked or fastened by bronze nails or clamps. After various bowings and scrapings to two deities on behalf of the town and people and the Brotherhood there is a curious injunction to have the 'usual jokes with the sheep', at least that would appear to be the meaning if the words signify what they would in Latin; but it may be that the word *ioca* in Iguvium meant rather 'exclamations' than anything humorous. It is certain that they were uttered over the head of the sheep; but if they were 'jokes', we may doubt if the sheep himself saw the point of them.

From this rather unsatisfactory guessing at the meaning of a number of difficult words, let us turn to a different (and surprising) source of information. In this very town of Gubbio on the 15th of May every year there is still held an extraordinary festival which does not appear to be, in fact, religious at all, at least not in any Christian sense, although it is recognised and patronised

---

[1] There is little doubt that it means 'at the full season of the second month'; only we do not know with which month the year began at Iguvium. If it was March, and began the year as at Rome, that would give us the end of April. But Ovid's list (*Fast.* 3. 94) shows that the second assumption is uncertain.

by the Bishop of the Diocese. It is called the Elevation of the *Ceri* and occupies the greater part of the day, and the best energies of three distinct bands, or crews, of men in gay uniform—white trousers, red shirts and caps, with a long string and tassel reaching to the waist, and a long coloured sash wound several times round the body. Each of these crews of men carry round the town one of the three *Ceri*, of which Figure 1 is a picture.

The *Cero* is carried on a wooden frame which ten men at a time are needed to bear, and the number of each crew is much larger than ten, so that they can take the duty in turn. The *Cero* itself is an erection of wood twelve feet high, divided in the middle by a kind of waist which unites an upper and a lower quasi-cylindrical case or box with rails projecting, giving to the octagon something like the look of a square. At the top of each of these *Ceri* there is erected the image of a saint, about two feet in height. The chief of the three is known as Saint Ubaldo, the famous Bishop of the town in the twelfth century, canonized in 1192. He is carried by a crew chosen from the Guild of Masons (*Muratori*). St George and St Antony are similarly represented at the top of the other two *Ceri*, carried by crews from the traders (*Negozianti*) and countrymen (*Contadini*) respectively. They make two circuits of the town by fixed routes, one in the morning and one in the evening, each *Cero* going separately, except at a fixed hour when they all meet in the central Piazza. All their movements are conducted at a run, even up quite steep ascents; but custom is merciful enough to allow them to pause for refreshment, mostly liquid, at the house of any patron who will provide a tub of wine, and secure for his house thereby all the advantages connected with the favour of the particular saint for the ensuing year. Wherever it is understood that the saint desires to show particular favour to a house, his crew, with their long and cumbrous stretcher on their shoulders, walk, or rather rush round, in the narrow street outside the house at least once, but sometimes three times, if neither the saint nor they get too giddy. Besides these private entertainments they are provided with an elaborate mid-day meal attended by the Bishop and other notables. Neither the Bishop nor any ecclesiastic shares in the procession; but after Vespers in the evening a kind of deputation headed by the Bishop and carrying the portrait of St Ubaldo, taken down from his proper home in his monastery, goes to meet the Ceri at a particular corner of the town. The picture of the saint is waggled to and fro, and his image at the top of the Cero makes an equally moving response. Then the Bishop and his reverend companions draw to one side, and the Ceri plunge off again at full speed down a steep hill. Finally the Ceri with the saints are rushed up another hill to a monastery at the top, to be taken care of for another year in a compartment labelled as belonging not to the monastery but to the town. It is quite clear that St Ubaldo has anticipated by many centuries the prevailing temper of the drivers of modern vehicles. Speed is essential to his happiness; safety does not matter. For when he arrives at the monastery he has nearly always lost most of his clothes, and on one recent occasion he had lost his head too. I have seen a cinematograph picture of the festival, from which it appears that the crews of the Ceri are highly popular and always accompanied on their round by an excited and enthusiastic following of citizens, old and young. Figure 1 shows the general appearance of the *Ceri* in the street. Figure 2 gives small models of the three which are preserved in the Municipal Museum. Figure 3 is a photograph of the quiet procession of ecclesiastics on their way to meet it. Figure 4 is from a painting preserved in the Municipal Museum, which the cinema picture entirely confirmed, of the scene in the Piazza. I owe these pictures and the description of the festival to a charming study of the ceremonies by Mr Herbert M. Bower.[1]

I have been tempted to dwell perhaps at greater length on this picturesque ceremony than its importance deserves; but the correspondence with what we were able to elicit from the ancient Iguvine Tables does, I think, suggest some historical connexion. The double peregrination of the town seems to point to the combination of two different ceremonies, and the extraordinary shape of the *Ceri* may perhaps correspond to the two storeys of the wicker framework with the victim in the third storey above or below the other two, which might be taken to explain in part the extraordinary structure of the *Ceri* at Gubbio on their stretcher.

But what has all this to do with modern religion? More than perhaps appears. Not in the features of the procession itself, but in at least two aspects, in which the ancient liturgy and the modern festival are thoroughly typical of the Italian religious outlook, the number (namely

[1] *The Elevation and Procession of the Ceri at Gubbio*, London, published for the Folk-Lore Society, 1897. I have never succeeded in visiting Gubbio on May 15; but my friend Mr Cyril Bailey tells me he saw it as recently as 1912 and has met friends who have seen it since 1918. I thank the Folk-Lore Society cordially for their kind permission to reproduce the pictures.

Fig. 1. The Ceri of Gubbio

Fig. 2. Models of the Ceri

Fig. 3. The procession of Ecclesiastics

Fig. 4. The scene in the Piazza of Gubbio

three) and nature of the deities worshipped together, the number being still observed in the modern festival, and the processional element in both. We shall be able to estimate the value of these things better after we have glanced briefly at a very different kind of deity who was worshipped by a different people in North Italy, a people, I suppose, who have contributed not less to the civilisation of the world, in ethics and in art, than the Umbrians, even though Umbria can claim the great dramatist Plautus, some famous painters, and, above all, St Francis: I mean the people called Venetians, who in ancient times can claim as wholly their own the historian Livy and at least the Italian part of the poet Vergil.

They had the city which we call Padua for their chief centre, famous in ancient times for the high character of its morals and for its worship of a goddess whom the Romans called Juno. We have learnt a little about them in the last twenty years from the study of the inscriptions in their own language, which was spoken in the whole north-eastern area of Italy before it was invaded by Latin, a process which only began in the second century B.C. This language we call Venetic, and it is in this that are written the dedications upon objects offered to the goddess Rehtia, whom the Romans identified with Juno. The chief centre of Rehtia's worship was a temple of considerable (but not at all magnificent) size at the little town which is now called Este, which students of the Middle Ages know as the home of the Guelfs, and hence one of the origins of our own royal family. This interesting cult is one of the many parts of ancient history which we owe entirely to the zeal of modern excavators, since it is never mentioned in any ancient writings and

you will not find Rehtia's name even in that vast store-
house of learning, the Encyclopaedia edited successively
by Pauly, Wissowa and Kroll. It has been my fortune
for many years past to study these remains, which in more
than one respect seem to mark an interesting factor in the
development of religion.

Notice first of all the name *Rehtia* which if it existed
in Latin would be *Rectia*, and that, being interpreted, is
'straightness'. This characteristic is very plain both in
the images of the goddess herself and in the style of
adornment regular upon the offerings she received from
her worshippers. In the pictures reproduced as Figures 5
and 6 you will see her style of dress. Notice the very
regular spiral lines in the upper part of the dress, and the
straight lines in the lower part; and in the little amulet,
which is very much like the charms which some of us
are wont to carry on our watch chains, notice the straight
lines of the crossed breastband and of the folds or trim-
ming on her sleeves. Notice also the projection of her
cap in front.

The objects disinterred from the ruins of her temple
show that she was interested in at least three classes of
offering. The first need not detain us long. The Veneti
were greatly interested in horse-racing and horse-breed-
ing, and the next illustration (Fig. 7) shows you a little
votive figure, which, however crude, is full of spirit,
and beside it the top of one of the pedestals with an
inscription which dedicated to Rehtia just such an image.
Unhappily time has left us nothing but the hinder hoofs,
imbedded in the plaster. Since her votaries were keenly
interested in horses, they naturally assumed that Rehtia
was too, and that the promise of such an offering would

Fig. 5. *Rehtia or her votaries*

Fig. 6. *Rehtia, image and talisman*

Fig. 7. *Equestrian offerings to Rehtia*

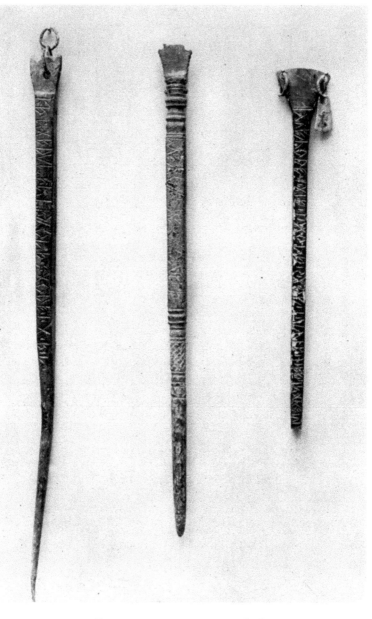

Fig. 8. *Votive pins, inscribed*

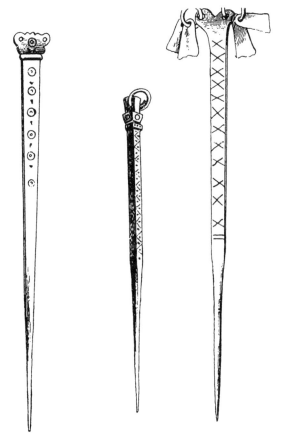

Fig. 9. *Votive pins with symbols*

Fig. 10. *Votive alphabetic tablet*

incline her to give victory to any horses whom they had entered for the race.

Secondly, we find among the offerings a very large number of objects which at first were called nails—some of them are shown in Figures 8 and 9. Even a glance at them will satisfy us that that description cannot be correct. Nails do not end in a thin plate with corners pierced by rings which hold small bell-shaped tablets. Their nature has been determined by my friend and former pupil, Professor Joshua Whatmough of Harvard, who by other examples of prophylactic, jingling ornaments of similar axe-head shape, from Venetia, Carinthia and the Eastern Alps, has shown[1] that they are neither more nor less than hairpins, long enough to be planted deeply in the lofty and solid coiffure which was the fashionable headdress of ladies in those days and regions, and was still known to the poet Juvenal some centuries later. The curious little objects that fluttered and tinkled at the free end of the pin were intended to avert any evil spirits who might otherwise be tempted to do harm to the owner of the pin through envy of her splendid head of hair or her other qualities. These pins are highly rectilinear. A cross is their commonest ornament, and even where they bear inscriptions these often end with a number of symbols, meaningless except for whatever signification their geometrical character may have implied.

The last of Rehtia's interests or amusements which we need to consider is the most interesting to us. Figure 10 shows one of the bronze tablets which were dedicated to her, of a peculiar kind. Some six of them are still fairly

[1] *Rehtia, the Venetic Goddess of Healing*, in the Journ. R. Anthrop. Institute, lii (1922), p. 219.

complete, and we have fragments of several more. Written upon them we always find three different types or divisions of the dedication. The most prominent is the word or symbol *akeo*, each of its letters written in a separate square, vertically one above the other, and each row of these four squares with the same letters repeated sixteen times. It is clear that Rehtia knew how to make a square, not merely by line but by arithmetic. Then all round the edge of the tablet, and sometimes on the body of it also, come the letters of the Venetic alphabet, first one by one, each in its own little pigeon-hole, which, however, is a small square, each attended by the two little vertical straight lines which are signs of accent in Venetic writing. Then the same letters, or at least the consonantal signs among them, repeated generally three times, combined with the signs for *r, n, l*, successively. For instance, *pr, pn, pl*, followed by *śr, śn, śl*, and so on. The third element in the inscription is the explicit dedication of the tablet, which is supposed to be speaking and calling itself 'me', declaring that 'so-and-so has presented me to Rehtia'. Very much the same remark is made in the inscriptions on the pins and on the pedestals of the horses.

Out of the many fascinating points which these curious objects suggest for discussion, I must only draw attention to one. Why did the votary, who is most commonly a woman, imagine that the goddess would be pleased to receive these highly alphabetic tokens of devotion? We do not know; but the most probable guess connects these tablets and several other votive alphabets from different parts of Italy on vases, but without any explicit dedication, with the use of the alphabet still preserved in the

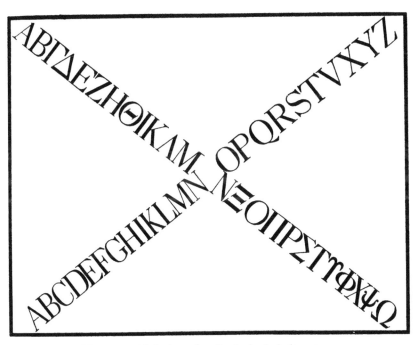

Fig. 11. *Alphabets for Cathedral-dedications*

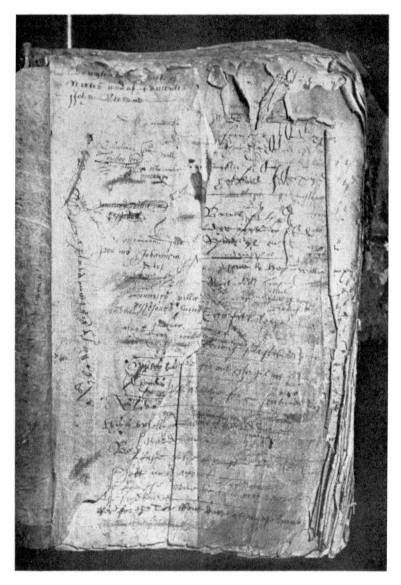

Fig. 12. Omen-guard in a church MS of 1599

consecration of Roman Catholic cathedrals.¹ After writing the two alphabets, Greek and Roman, diagonally across the floor of the church with his pastoral staff in a bed of ashes, starting from each of two corners of the new cathedral, as is shown by the pattern (Fig. 11), the consecrating Pontifex utters two exorcisms, one for 'expelling all temptations of the demons', and the other for 'expelling the devil lest he be found in any shady place (*umbraculis*) of this church'. The same custom is still preserved in a greatly abbreviated form, in the dedication of Anglican cathedrals. In England we are content if the dedicating Bishop writes the letters alpha and omega in a circle of sand, which is then swept away. But in Roman Catholic cathedrals the whole Greek alphabet and the Latin are still employed for this picturesque purpose, as the figure shows.

After this essay was written I received an interesting piece of evidence of the survival of this use of the alphabet for what may be called an Omen-guard, in an English document dated 1599, from my friend the Rev. Harold Cavalier, M.A., Vicar of St Stephen's, St Albans. He kindly allows me to reproduce here (Fig. 12) a photograph (of the fragment of the first leaf lying upon the second) of the Churchwardens' Book of Brington, Northamptonshire, bearing that date. The only thing

¹ See A. Dieterich, *Kleine Schriften* (Leipzig, 1911, pp. 202 ff.) and the following article. For the Roman Catholic use he quotes from the *Pontificale Romanum*, revised by Popes Benedict XIV and Leo XIII in 1891, p. 130; the instructions are identical in the edition of 1862, which the curious may find in the British Museum Library (shelf 2010C). In the same article will be found also an interesting account of the Sicilian Abbizzè, a half-sacred, half-magical tract, dropped into a new-born baby's cradle, some of the charms consisting of portions of the alphabet, whence its name.

which concerns us[1] is the alphabet written irregularly at the side with what appear to be three varieties of the first letter, two capitals, one minuscule, and continuing thus: b c d e f g h i k l m[2] n o p q r s t u. Then follow a number of curious scrawls which might be described as attempts at *w*; but which, I think, like the large A's at the beginning, are to be regarded rather as the attempts of a man knowing little Greek to produce a Greek ω. He seems to have crossed out five attempts and to have satisfied himself with the sixth.

There seems little doubt that this was an ancient way of excluding from the use of the alphabet all evil spirits, especially the Devil. The word to *spell* originally meant to 'make a charm'; and the art of writing, in communities where it was a novelty, was naturally looked on with suspicion and even dread. The person who could write possessed a power uncannily greater than anything which might be devised by a person who could not.

Space forbids me to linger even on these vestiges of so interesting a person as the Devil. What I am concerned to suggest is perfectly obvious from these monuments and will involve us in no Mediaeval problems. The people who made these offerings, whatever their object, had at least a strong claim upon the sympathy and gratitude of the despised class of society in which my more active years were spent, I mean that of professors.

---

[1] Though the initial statement and prayer which will be seen as the first entry in the column are worth a glance: *Gulielmus Sám*(?) *Traceloe scri(psit). Deus propissius esto mihi peccatori.*

[2] *m* and *n* between them have one stroke too many which is marked for deletion apparently by two dots above and below the first stroke of the *m*. Then the *o* is very small and its right hand side is obscured by what seems an accidental stroke.

Gratitude because their efforts have recorded for us the facts of Venetic writing which enable us to read with certainty all the other inscriptions in this little known dialect, and sympathy because they obviously believed with all their hearts in the value of having things written down and correctly spelt. In other words, the goddess Rehtia was really a literary character, and particular to have even the accents of her words rightly recorded. The only other point which can be called probably certain about these tablets is that the word *akeo*, written vertically and repeated sixteen times, means either 'heal us' or 'O Lady Healer'.

It is worth noting in illustration of this literary taste, not so very common, if you come to think of it, among the deities of antiquity, that another goddess, either a daughter or sister of Rehtia, or Rehtia herself with a new name *Louzera* corresponding to the Latin *Libera*, who was worshipped in the northern part of the Venetic area, in the valley where Titian was born some sixteen centuries later, has a standing epithet, a word which seems to mean 'blest by the Muses', 'educated', or 'learned'.[1] In Latin the phrase would be *Libera musicata*. One could hardly have invented, if one had tried, three names better

[1] Since I wrote this I have come across the fact that the Latin deity or deities, *Carmenta* or *Carmentis*, with the epithets *postvorta* (Varro ap. Gell. 16. 16; Macrob. 1. 7. 20, if, as seems likely, he is referring to the same deities; Ovid, *Fast.* 1. 633) and *prorsa* (Varro, l.c.), *antevorta* (Macrob. l.c.) or *porrima* (Ovid, l.c.), was a goddess of birth, as these epithets sufficiently show. Do they denote companions or, more probably, were they originally epithets of Lucina? See Warde Fowler, *Religious Experience of the Roman People*, p. 297. The resemblance in the meaning of *Carmenta* and *Musicata* is striking, and I find it hard to dismiss it as accidental. If it is a real parallel, then the 'learning' of Louzera will be like that of Carmenta, namely a knowledge of charms for ensuring the safe birth of children.

fitted to typify the features of the great Venetian race than these three implying 'rectitude', 'freedom' and 'the friendship of the Muses'.

Any Greek scholars who may read these pages will have long since recognised, in this Venetic goddess at the head of the Adriatic, the counterpart of a Greek goddess of whom also we have learnt much from recent excavation, this time on Greek soil at Sparta, but who is also mentioned several times by Greek authors, especially the poet Pindar. I mean the goddess Orthia, or Orthosia, 'straightness' or 'straightening', a meaning too close to that of Rehtia to allow us to doubt that the two deities must, at one time or other, have been the same. Here are one or two pictures (Fig. 13) of Orthia from her shrine at Sparta, which will show you that she too was fond of straight lines and crosses. We know from Pindar that her chief duty in Boeotia was to restore women to health after childbirth, but at Sparta, as perhaps one might expect, she took a more masculine sphere. Besides chariot-racing and other sports, she patronised in the time of Cicero what was known as the Contest of Endurance, in which boys competed with one another in their power of standing stiff or holding out under the lash,[1] and it is recorded that more than one succumbed under the ordeal. There is no hint of any literary interest

---

[1] It has recently been pointed out by Miss Jocelyn Toynbee (*J. Rom. Stud.* xix. 1929, p. 81, following Thomsen, *Archiv Rel. Wiss.* 1906, p. 397) that the statement of Pausanias (8. 23. 1) about this flagellation of the ἔφηβοι at Sparta at Orthia's temple seems to be connected with the use of this gruesome rite as a charm to produce fertility. Orthia, therefore, as well as Rehtia, seems to have been interested in bringing children into the world; though the goddess in Italy shows no sign of any kind of cruelty.

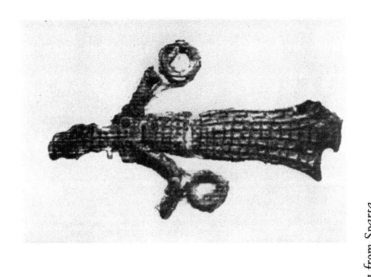

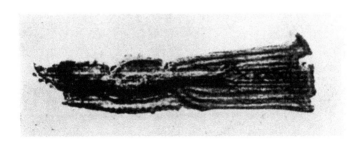

Fig. 13. *Images of Orthia from Sparta*

Fig. 14. Minoan Nature-goddess from Cnossos and the Sacred Cow

here, though we observe the same connexion with healing as Rehtia's inscriptions testified.

Finally, I must bid you leap across the sea, and across
many centuries backward in time, into Minoan Crete.
Here are two pictures (Fig. 14) of the image of the nature-
goddess who was worshipped with great devotion at
Cnossos. Observe the straight lines and squares on her
skirt and on her apron, and the rigidity of her flounces.
Observe further, what is to me conclusive evidence of
her kinship with Rehtia, the ornamentation of her tall
headdress; you see that it is spiral, and ends in a small
projection over the front of the tall hat, just as Rehtia's
did. But if you look further into the picture of this
Cretan goddess—who is still without a name, because
we cannot decipher the signs in which the language of
Minos was written—you will see that what she is wearing
is neither more nor less than a snake, whose head looks
out above her own, no doubt to assure the worshipper
that this goddess could completely control the snakes,
as well as the other wild creatures, such as the lions who
are often represented as her attendants. The next picture
is also associated with her worship, as well as with
Egypt; and it may be the astrological lore of Egypt, as
Sir Arthur Evans conjectures, that was the source of the
star-like ornament which appears on this sacred cow.
But I mention it now merely as showing a possible origin
for the crosses of which Rehtia is so fond. It would
seem, at all events, that Rehtia's earlier history lay in
Greece and perhaps in Crete.

Now if I have not wearied you too much with these
objects of primitive worship, let me point out briefly
the kind of influence that these two cults, Venetic and

Umbrian, represent in the religion of Ancient Italy. I may express them briefly in three considerations. I am referring, be it observed, to Italy, not to Greece or to Minoan Crete.

First, although in one sense it is clear that the deities were local, that is not true in the narrowest sense. We hear nothing, it is true, of Praestita and Tursa except at Gubbio; but on the other hand their worship is not connected with a particular corner of a particular shrine. No doubt they were housed somewhere, like the *Ceri* of Gubbio, for the greater part of the year. But on their great day or days they come out, out into the open air, out all round the town, out even into individual houses of citizens. You may call their images fetishes, if you like, in the sense that they have a sanctity of their own; but they are not fetishes in the sense of being tied up to a particular tree or a particular rock. They move, they run, they dance, and, so far as their wooden limitations allow them, they eat and drink and feast. At all events their sympathy with their worshippers in doing all these things is manifestly declared.

The truth is, though I do not know that it has often been pointed out, that the Processional element[1] in religious ceremonies has a certain definitely religious value. Of course it is popular—everybody can join in, everybody can watch, everybody can enjoy the dances and the dresses and the other good things; but somewhere behind all these obvious attractions there does definitely lie the conception that the object of worship is in rela-

---

[1] We do not know enough about Rehtia to be sure of this point in her programme; but the remains at Este include lines of figures dressed alike, which would seem to warrant us in supposing that some kind of a procession was part of her ritual.

tion to other people than his or her priest, and to more of the world than is contained in the most gorgeous altar or the most hallowed shrine. Am I wrong in thinking that this processional element in religion, which we all recognise as especially characteristic of the form of Christianity which Italy handed on to the rest of Europe, is, after all, a matter which should interest serious students of religion? It has certainly interested some of the chief advocates of religion in our own day. I am not thinking merely of the beautiful processions of children which the Roman Catholic Church still organises in many of our northern towns at Whitsuntide; I am thinking also of those humbler but perhaps even more interesting processions by which the Salvation Army has carried its Faith into hundreds of dark streets and thousands of squalid homes.

Secondly, a student of language must be pardoned for dwelling on the names of these Italian deities. You observe they are feminine in gender, and it is quite true that this has often led, especially in districts under Greek influence in South Italy, to the worship of deities definitely of female sex. You may see the development even in the small number of figures of Rehtia which I have been able to show. Only the latest can be said to have definitely female characteristics, though down in the South, among the Minoans, there is no doubt that the goddess whom they worshipped was from the beginning every inch a mother. But there is a curious fact in the history of language which is closely connected with the abstract and impersonal conception of deity widely spread over Ancient Italy. We have seen the meaning of the three names 'Straightness', 'Helping', 'Terrifying', and we shall find later on that deities of this kind are by no means strange to the old Italian peoples. Now behind all these lies what I may call a grammarian's secret. What we call the suffixes proper to the feminine gender had, in Greek and Latin and all the kindred tongues, to start with, nothing to do with sex. They all denoted some such collective or abstract idea as the names of the deities we have been noting—*fuga* 'flight', *senecta* 'old age', *iuuentus* 'youth' or 'the collection of men of military age', and dozens more. My second point therefore comes to this, that these early deities of Italy, though feminine, were not necessarily female, nor even quite personal, though under later influences they became so.

Closely akin to this is my third and last point, and we may perhaps connect it, in passing, with the number in each group of the deities at Iguvium, sometimes two, more often three. Enough has already been said to show that men's conception of the objects of their worship in Ancient Italy may generally be described as functional. He or she existed in order to do a particular thing, whether an operation of nature or a service to man, and each of them had properly his or her own sphere, so that they did not generally get in each other's way—though of course your own deities would resist any deities whom your enemies might be able to influence in their own favour. One consequence of this was a process very familiar to every student of ancient literature, I mean the ease with which two deities of more or less similar functions could be rolled into one. Neptune, the god of waters in Italy, fresh water as well as salt, could not well deny his likeness to Poseidon, the Greek god of the sea; though poor Poseidon would have been very uncomfortable in a small

Italian lake of fresh water where there was hardly room for him to use his trident, and which might even be much hotter than he liked. The stately Rehtia, of course, could be identified with the matron Juno. Traces of this extraordinary habit of mind are abundant on every page of Latin inscriptions. I should not like to have to count the number of deities with whom the (more or less) worthy Augustus,[1] of whatever date, was ultimately identified in different places. I am anxious here only to insist upon the fact that lies behind all this, namely that to the Italian mind the particular object of worship was in essence not a person but merely an entity which performed a certain function.

In passing I must point out, for I can do no more, how closely related this frame of mind is to that which maintains no small number of saints in the Roman Church to-day, who have special sanctity only in special places where they are believed to dispense miraculous blessings. One form of this is the large number of sub-titles attached to the Virgin Mary, like " Our Lady of Walsingham" in Norfolk; " Notre Dame de Lourdes"; " Notre Dame de la Garde" at Marseilles, whose church is full of votive images of ships which she is reputed to have saved.

[1] He begins by being counted one of the Lares (as Horace recognised), and he is often called Hercules or Neptune or Apollo, or by the name of some local deity, in a multitude of inscriptions. Now and then it is difficult to be sure that Augustus, so to speak, is all there, because in some cases it seems as if his name was only added to that of a local deity to give that deity a kind of orthodox political flavour. Hercules—yes; but an Augustean Hercules, so that the worshipper may get the benefit of whatever human or supra-human blessings the use of both names might bring him. And such creatures as *Nymphae Augustae* cannot well be the Emperor in person! A whole chapter might be written, or many chapters—no doubt many have been—on this process of the amalgamation of deity. For the Orphic view of the matter see p. 36.

Thus you would not have been surprised if you had penetrated one day with me far into the Abruzzi on the shores of what used to be Lake Fucinus, and had been presented by the local Abbot with a liturgy in regular use, written and chanted in honour of two local saints, Rufino and Cesidio, who are greatly sought after, especially on their own day of the year, namely August 11, because of their peculiar but locally well-known function of curing scrofula and diseases of the throat. The first stanza of the hymn in their honour runs as follows:

> Si gutturis contagia
> Strumaeque luem improbam
> Vitare in aevum expetis
> Caesidii nomen invoca.[1]

This is taken from a pamphlet published at Avezzano in 1885, and presented to me in 1894 with pride by the author, the Abbot D. de Vincentiis.

And with these things in your mind you will perhaps regard with more tolerance the British farmer who is said to have replied to one of his comforters, 'Yes, a' do know God A'mighty be good and merciful; but that there Providence do seem to have a spite agin me'. Let me leave with you, then, one quite serious question. Did not this Italian habit, of recognising special functions in special divine entities, contribute at least some of the material to the great edifice of belief, perhaps the most imposing ever set up by that force of speculative reason

[1]   If from contagious throat-disease
            And scrofulous decay
        You'd flee for ever, on your knees
            To Saint Cesidio pray—

a simple enough prescription, in Latin or in English; perhaps even worthy of the late Mrs Eddy.

called, I believe, Constructive Theology, an edifice built into its final shape by the philosophers of the Roman Church, the doctrine of the Trinity, the conception of a Supreme Being who is, in a mystic sense, Three as well as One, and One as well as Three?

These are high matters on which one who is neither philosopher nor theologian can offer no more than a question. But we shall not have wasted our time if these pictures can afford a conception of how some of the early peoples of Italy thought about the objects of their worship, and how some of their thoughts have helped to shape our own world.

CHAPTER II

ORPHEUS IN ITALY

THE title of this essay may seem strange, since Orpheus is familiar to all of us as the hero of a beautiful and tragic myth which, like his name, we are accustomed to attribute to Greek sources. Orpheus and Eurydice, one supposes, must both be Greek; and did he not come from Thrace? Did he not descend to fetch his wife from the Underworld through one of its famous mouths on Greek soil, the cave of Mount Taenarus? Did he not meet his death on the great river of Thrace, the Hebrus? What has he to do with Italy? That is a question which might naturally be asked by any schoolboy who had read the story told in the Fourth Book[1] of Vergil's *Georgics*, and it is one which must be answered.

First we must acknowledge one sad truth, though nowadays it will hardly be surprising. Just as Betsy Prig shocked Mrs Gamp by declaring that there was "no sich a person" as the famous "Mrs 'Arris", so Aristotle,[2] in his brief way, assures us that the poet Orpheus never existed.

Suidas[3] tells us that there were at least five persons

---

[1] Although, as we know from Servius, it was really an earlier poem put into that Book to make up for its original conclusion, destroyed because of a political tragedy.

[2] Quoted by Cicero, *Nat. Deor.* 1. 38. 108.

[3] See Kern, *Orphicorum Fragmenta*, p. 64. 223, from Diels, *Vorsokr.* II³, 163. 1.

who used the name, six, if you count as two one person who is given a double origin; and out of these five, four are described as having written epic poems. Two of the five are comparatively well-known people, Orpheus of Croton in South Italy, who is mentioned as a friend of Pisistratus, the great tyrant of Athens in 560 B.C., and Orpheus of Camarina in Sicily, who wrote a 'Descent into Hell'. One more is said to have come from Arcadia or from Kikone in Thrace, and one more from another part of Thrace (Odrysae), and one from Macedonia (Leibethra).

Any one who may be familiar with the tradition given by Pindar in his Fourth Pythian will perhaps think that, at all events, Orpheus must have been as real a person as Jason, because he went with the Argonauts; but we cannot allow him even this degree of reality without question; for a most respectable critic, Pherecydes, of the fifth century B.C., tells us that it was not Orpheus, but somebody called Philammon who went with Jason. In short, if one puts together all the legends about Orpheus, one feels that it is they and not the Thracian Bacchants that have really torn him into small pieces. The truth is that the name Orpheus seems to have been a kind of professional epithet like " Doctor" or " Reverend", applied to persons who wrote poems on Orphic subjects, which were always of a religious character. I cannot suppose that the last word has been said about the growth of this religion; for if, as seems pretty certain, there was no one person called Orpheus to found it, who did found it, and where? And how did he or they learn its substance, and whence? From Egypt or from further East? There seems much to be said for thinking with L. von

Schroeder and Furtwängler[1] that the ethical essence of the Orphic doctrine was due to Pythagoras, drawing from Indian sources.

There is, however, no doubt that the story of Orpheus grew up on Greek soil. But in the sixth century B.C. and later we must remember that Greek soil included a multitude of active and wealthy cities in Italy and Sicily, so that that region was known by the name of Greater Greece; and recent study seems to have made it certain that the roots of this Orphic religion, at all events those which took most kindly to life, were not in the mainland of Greece, still less in Thrace, but deeply set in South Italy. The legends of a personal founder of that religion were gradually developed in the hands of many verse writers who were adherents of the Orphic cult. Besides the two who actually called themselves Orpheus, in Croton and in Camarina respectively, we know of four other poets from Greater Greece[2] who wrote on Orphic subjects. We know from Pindar[3] that Theron, tyrant of Agrigentum, was connected with the Orphic religion, and Pausanias[4] tells us that a statue of Orpheus was erected at Olympia by Mikythos of Rhegium, who was banished in 476 B.C. from Sicily; and Pausanias in that passage describes Orpheus as 'the Thracian'. If that name actually was on the statue, it was the earliest mention of his connexion with Thrace. This is a dull

---

[1] *Ant. Gemmen*, iii (1900), p. 262, footn. 2; p. 263, footn. 4.

[2] Timocles of Syracuse, Zopyros of Heraclea, Nikias of Elea, and Brontinus of Metapontum, besides the Pythagorean philosopher Kerkops, who wrote another κατάβασις and a ἱερὸς λόγος, which may be the one that Herodotus (2. 81) speaks of. See O. Kern, *Orpheus* (1920), p. 3.

[3] *Olymp.* 2. 56–80, dating from 476 B.C.

[4] 5. 26. 3.

list; but it seemed necessary to show how strong is the evidence connecting the very beginnings of the legend with Italy rather than with Greece in the narrower sense; and it is quite certain, as we shall see, that the great spread of the Orphic religion took place in Italy, where it has left behind peculiar and interesting documents, some of which we will examine.

The German scholar Otto Kern, to whose treatise on Orpheus (1920), with his admirable collection of the Orphic Fragments (1922), I am greatly indebted, has shown that there are at least three different stages in the development of what we may call the Orpheus-myth. The central and most universal conception of him is that he was an inspired singer or poet, for the two terms were used, as we all know, interchangeably in Greek and Latin writers; and that his song was so much more power-ful than that of ordinary singers as to give him miraculous power over objects of nature, birds and beasts, and rocks and trees, who were all subdued by the beauty of his song. That is Orpheus in his first shape, and with this Kern and others very plausibly connect the derivation of his name, which they link with the Greek word ὀρφανός[1] (Latin orbus), to mean a solitary person who loved to live in the deserts or wild mountain valleys; and the name of his father Oeagros, which properly means 'the man of the lonely field', suggests the same connexion.

Next, however, comes a feature in the story which is certainly closely connected with the nature of the Orphic rites. These mysteries were concerned with preparation

[1] The evidence of the story of the cult seems to me to support this derivation better than one which I was taught by the late Professor E. B. Cowell, connecting it with the Sanskrit word ṛbhu-, 'a poet, wizard, or clever elf'. But the two do not seem necessarily inconsistent.

for the life of the Underworld; and people who were initiated into them on earth were encouraged to expect great advantages after death. The subject of most of the poems connected with the sect seems to have been the nature of the world below. Several of them are entitled Katabasis, that is, the descent into the Lower World. Now if the followers of Orpheus wrote like this, it is obvious that they would attribute to their supposed master, as we know they did, special knowledge of the infernal regions, and a personal visit to them by himself might well be a poetical expression of this. But here comes the saddest part of my confession.

In none of the earliest accounts of that journey, nor indeed in any of the fragments of the Orphic literature proper, is there any mention of the wife of Orpheus; and when she does appear, some authors call her Eurydice, and some call her Agriope; and none of the earlier of these leaves any doubt in our minds that Orpheus succeeded in getting her back alive. Thus Hermesianax (who flourished about 300 B.C.) says definitely, in a fragment of 14 lines preserved by Athenaeus,[1] that by his singing Orpheus persuaded the great lords of the Underworld to let Agriope 'win the breath of soft life' (μαλακοῦ πνεῦμα λαβεῖν βιότου). Even Plato,[2] though he prudently opines that it was only a ghost that Orpheus saw and not the real wife, gives no hint whatever of his having failed through his looking back. So it appears that the whole pretty story which Vergil has made immortal, and Gluck, in the eighteenth century, set to famous music, was the invention of the Hellenistic Age, somewhere, that is, in the third or second century B.C.; and seeing the

[1] 13. 597b.   [2] *Sympos.* 179d.

close connexion between Sicily and Alexandria and the abundance and popularity of Orphic writings in South Italy and Sicily, Kern can hardly be wrong in concluding that the story was invented there and not in Greece proper at all.

Thirdly, we have the tragic legend of the death of Orpheus in Thrace after his expedition to the Under-world. Here there is another definite link between the legend and the Orphic religion, which was pointed out by as early an authority as Proklos,[1] the ancient com-mentator on Plato. Writing in the times of the new Platonists, who made a good deal of Orphism, Proklos points out that Orpheus, having become the leader of the mysterious rites of Dionysus, is said to have suffered the same fate as did that deity, namely of being torn in pieces; and we know that Aeschylus, in his play of the *Bassarides*, represents Orpheus as a Greek who preached and sang of Apollo to the Thracians and was torn to pieces by Thracian Bacchants who were worshipping Dionysus. It appears to have been a drama in which Aeschylus de-picted, and no doubt confirmed, a reconciliation in re-ligion. Just as in the *Oresteia* he reconciled the worship of Athena with the older worship of the Eumenides, so in this Thracian trilogy of the *Lykurgeia* he used the death of Orpheus as an incident in reconciling the more or less competing claims of Apollo and Dionysus.

But I must not dwell upon the Greek side[2] of Orphism

[1] *In Remp.* 398 (W. Kroll, Teubner, 1899, i. p. 174).
[2] For an interesting account of this side of the question I am indebted to a lecture on *Orphic Literature and Doctrine*, by Prof. J. F. Dobson of Bristol (privately printed for the London Branch of the Classical Association, 1919). "Homer", he observes, "knew no Purgatory, whereas Orpheus knew no Hell."

for, as a Byzantine scholar pathetically remarked 900 years ago, 'it is impossible to get to the end of them'; and the fate of several eminent scholars in recent years who have embarked on this almost uncharted sea of speculation about prehistoric religion in Greece is a sufficient warning to any less qualified person. The evidence from Italy, however, so far as it goes, is concrete, less ancient, and not difficult to date; and it has a direct bearing on religious history.

From the first the teachers of Orphism in Italy were what we should call highly moral. They believed in a kind of conditional immortality which was attained either by a life of purity on earth or, in the end, by processes of purification in the after-life. Vergil's well-known account of this purgation represents the Orphic traditions fairly closely and resembles that of Plato, save that it is free from the curious arithmetical and astronomical stamp which it received in the teaching of two great mathematicians, Pythagoras and Plato; but as early as the time of Plato[1] there had been built into Orphism what Charles Kingsley called 'those comfortable back-stairs',[2] that is, a short cut into Heaven, to be obtained, not indeed without trouble, but by ascetic discipline on earth under the direction and, mostly, the well-remunerated direction, of Orphic priests. In the next essay some evidence will be given for believing that the Etruscans proceeded still further to debase this doctrine by supposing that a man's fortunes in Purgatory could be affected by sacrifices and offerings made on earth, even after his death, by persons acting on his behalf.[3] But the accounts we have elsewhere

---

[1] *Republic,* 2. 364 (e).
[2] *The Water Babies,* ch. viii.
[3] See p. 60.

of Orphism do not suggest that the orthodox initiate in that faith could rely on any other performance than his own. Yet how popular the Orphic " back-stairs" were in South Italy, at all events among the wealthy, we know from some remarkable evidence which has been discovered in recent years.

There is first the epitaph of the fifth century B.C. from Cumae, in which the initiate boldly declares, if this reading of the inscription[1] can be trusted, that since he has

[1] See Sogliano, *Not. Scav.* 1905, ii. p. 377, who describes the stone as having a shape which shows that it was the lid of a tomb: ου θεμις εντουθα κεισθαιι με τον βεβαχχευμενον. His interpretation seems to me reasonably certain, as to the editors of the 1925 Liddell and Scott; the only possible point of doubt is a superfluous stroke (κεισθαιι instead of κεισθαι). But to regard this as a contraction of κεῖσθαι with a following εἰ and render 'no one but an initiate must occupy this tomb', as Otto Hoffmann (Bechtel-Collitz, *Samml. Griech. Dial. Inschrr.* iv. p. 85) proposed, seems to me wildly improbable, in substance (for tombs were not commonly used by any save members of the household of the person first interred), and still more in language; can any other example of such a contraction in prose be produced? It is true that Wissowa, whose opinion on all matters of ancient religion commands high respect, assumed that the stone did not belong to a particular grave, but either to a large chamber or vault or enclosed area, and quoted one similar example from Rome which the editors of the Corpus (C.I.L. vi. 10412) take as possibly the monument of a Christian, and for which they accept Rossi's date, based on the style of the lettering, as belonging to the end of the second century A.D. This inscription tells us that the *monumentum* was built for the freedmen and freedwomen of certain persons with Graeco-Roman names *at* (i.e. *ad*) *religionem pertinentes meam*; and adds that a space of two feet all the way round outside the monument belongs to it. The inscription that precedes it (vi. 10411) is obviously one of the same class, because it ends with the words *religionis homines*, and says that the man who built it (T. Aelius Victorinus) has built it as a sacred place (*locus religiosus*) for the burial of their bodies. Now these inscriptions, found in Rome, are of a date at which there is at least considerable doubt as to what *religio* means; and in any case, they are six centuries and a half later than our inscription from Cumae. Further, we know about them, what at Cumae is at least doubtful, that they related to a monument or area in which there was room for many interments; and thirdly, the authors of these inscriptions express themselves in positive, not negative terms. It appears to me, therefore, that while on the

been initiated, it is forbidden by the law of Heaven (θέμις) that he should lie in the grave. Besides this we have a whole series of documents[1] discovered in the extreme south of Italy on the sites of Thurii and Petelia, two of which are now in the British Museum. In the Gold Ornament Room of the Graeco-Roman Department there are two bits of gold leaf or gold plate (numbered 3154 and 3155 respectively) covered with writing scratched upon them; and beside one of them is a gold necklace to which is attached the little cylindrical box in which the gold leaf was found folded up, the whole having come from a tomb (see Fig. 15).

What are these curious objects? They were clearly worn on the person, in life, death and burial. And since they were written on gold, it is also clear that they were dearly cherished; but it is obvious that no poor person need apply for one.[2] The earliest of these cannot possibly be dated later, from the form of the letters, than 300 B.C.; and, as we shall see, some go down into the Christian period.

What is written upon them varies. Some of them have

religious side, the interpretation of the Cumae inscription may be regarded as open to a certain doubt, it is best to trust to the distinct linguistic evidence and accept Sogliano's interpretation, unless and until another example is produced from the fifth century B.C. of such an extraordinary contraction as Hoffmann supposes, or of the single letter ι being written with the meaning of ει.

[1] The text of those translated in what follows, and my own reading of the two in the British Museum, with some comments on Prof. Gilbert Murray's reading, will be found in the John Rylands Library Bulletin for January, 1933, in an Appendix to this lecture, there printed in the form in which it was delivered in Manchester on Dec. 7, 1932.

[2] Plato, in his scornful description of the practices of persons professing to be in possession of Orphic secrets (*Rep.* 2. 363 (b)–364 (e)), says that they went about hawking their magical charms 'at rich men's doors'.

Fig. 15. *Gold necklace and case for Orphic certificate*

no particular reference to the candidate for immortality, who took them with him or with her (mostly with her, I suspect) to the grave; they simply recited some part of the story of Proserpine, whose annual resurrection was regarded in the Orphic teaching as a type of what an Orphic worshipper might look for. One of these[1] was found in 1879 on the site of the ancient Thurii. It is very difficult to read, largely because it is written in the magical fashion with a considerable number of repeated words; but the careful restoration by Diels[2] is very probable and makes good sense. It runs thus:

To Earth, the first mother of all, thus spake[3] the daughter of Cybele: O Sun, O Fire, thou takest thy way through all the cities, when thou hast appeared in Victories and Chances and Fate, the supreme disposer; with whom thou dost make rich thy gardens in thy sovereignty, O famous god; by thee all things are tamed and all are mastered, and all are filled with the lightning of fire. Everywhere decrees of Fate must be endured. Do thou, O Fire, take me to my mother if I have learnt to endure fasting and to pass seven nights and days fasting without food. In thy honour I passed seven days without food, O Zeus of Olympus, Zeus that seest all, O Sun.

[There follow two or three broken lines in which it would seem that she prays to be delivered (or declares that she has been delivered) from the 'fiery flood' and from the 'plain of Rhadamanthus'.]

I have given this interesting fragment in an absolutely literal prose version. The most striking feature of it is thoroughly characteristic of Orphic teaching, their per-

[1] Kern, *Orphicorum Fragmenta*, Berlin, 1922, Fragment 47.
[2] *Vorsokratiker*, vol. ii. ed. 3, 177, No. 21. I omit the lines which are hopelessly mutilated.
[3] There follows a broken line in which she mentions Demeter and all-seeing Zeus; and although the speech is represented as addressed to her mother, she in fact calls upon the Sun in the line which follows the break.

sistent attempt to identify[1] all the gods. Thus at the beginning of this extract Proserpine is called the daughter
of Cybele; but she addresses Earth as her mother, and
refers also to Demeter and Zeus. Then she turns to the
Sun, whom she identifies with Fire, and apparently pro-
ceeds to identify All-seeing Zeus of Olympus with him
too; and it certainly seems as if Victories and Chances
and Fate, who help the Sun to beautify his gardens, cannot be far removed from being identified with him.
Macrobius (1. 18. 18, and indeed the whole chapter) and
other authorities preserve for us what seems to have been
a favourite maxim of the Orphic ritual, a single line of
jingle which may be rendered 'Zeus and Pluto both are
one, one with Bacchus and the Sun', and another version
includes the Egyptian Sarapis in place of Bacchus. Among
other things, Macrobius points out that Vergil recognises[2]
the identification of Bacchus and Ceres with the Sun and
Moon in the exordium of the *Georgics* (i. 7):

> Vos, O clarissima mundi
> Lumina, labentem caelo quae ducitis annum,
> Liber et alma Ceres, uestro si munere tellus
> Chaoniam pingui glandem mutauit arista.

Note the Vergilian 'if'. In the fourth essay we shall trace
more fully the effect of these amalgamations.

Now come back to the fourth century B.C., and turn

---

[1] Euripides had complete sympathy with this attempt, as appears from
a striking passage in the *Helena*, 1302–40, where he calls Demeter the
mother of the gods and of Zeus, and concludes by praising the power
of the Bacchic orgies (1364). The reference I owe to Dr L. R. Farnell
in Hastings' *Encycl. of Rel. and Ethics*. Euripides was followed by Aratus
(*Phaen.* ll. 2–5), from the fifth line of which Paul quoted in his sermon
at Athens τοῦ γὰρ καὶ γένος ἐσμέν.

[2] But in his own undogmatic way, leaving any reader who likes to
take the names in coordination, not apposition, with *lumina* (cf. p. 90)
and leaving in doubt even their responsibility for having enabled men
to cultivate corn and the vine.

to what may be called documents with more practical
objects—though unpractical enough from our modern
point of view. If the fragment from Thurii which I have
rendered may be called a quotation from the narrative
portion of the Orphic Scriptures, the documents that
we are now to examine may be compared to certificates
of baptism, though they have been called 'Passports to
Heaven', as they are in intention. They also are of gold
and belong to much the same period as the Thurii tablet.
The earliest[1] of them, even allowing for intentional
archaism, can hardly be later than the fourth century B.C.

Let us take three examples in their chronological order.
The first I have made up from two tablets from Thurii, of
very similar purport (32 (e) and 32 (c) in Kern's *Fragmenta*), which happen to be mutilated, one at the end
and one soon after the beginning, so that they complement
each other quite well. In both of them the initiated soul
speaks herself, and she is of the feminine gender:

32 (e).   Pure, I come from the pure, O Queen of the Kingdom below,
           Hermes and Pluto and all; bear witness to that which ye know.
           For I can boast to belong to the same happy race as do ye,
           And for aught that was wrong in my deeds I have paid the full
               price to be free.
           .   .   .   .

32 (c).   As on wings I have soared far out from the treadmill of toil and
               of pain,
           And eagerly rising I entered the beautiful garden again.
           Safe I lay hid in the womb of our Queen that ruleth below,
           Till forth from the beautiful garden[2] she suffered me eager to go.
           Like a lamb that has plunged in the milk-pail I joyed in their
               welcome to me,
           'O blessed, O happy, no longer a mortal, but god thou shalt be'.

    [1] 32 (c) in Kern's collection (641. 1 in Kaibel, *Inscc. Graecae Ital. et
Sic.*); it shows, for instance, the single sign o for o, ω and ου.
    [2] The mystical image which I have rendered by 'beautiful garden',
ἱμερτὸς στέφανος, which the soul says she has first entered and then
left, having meanwhile hidden ὑπὸ κόλπον of Proserpine, is taken by

The curious comparison in the last sentence I take to
embody a shepherd's proverb for a misfortune unex-
pectedly turning to great good, and the reference to the
'treadmill' (Greek κύκλος) four lines before implies the
characteristic Orphic doctrine of purification through a
long cycle of human existences, each followed by a period
of purgation; 'longa dies perfecto temporis orbe' as
Vergil puts it.

The next, written probably between 300 and 200 B.C.,
comes from the ancient Petelia, one of the two in the
British Museum which I have already described. Its style
is, on the whole, more dignified than that of those I have
just rendered, and this I have tried to indicate by a different
metre. Prof. Gilbert Murray (in the Appendix to Dr Jane
Harrison's *Prolegomena*, p. 661) says quite justly: "the
dialect is pure literary epic".

> By Pluto's Palace, on the left, thou'lt see
> A stream beside a white-leaved cypress tree.
> From that stream guard thyself and draw not near;
> Another thou shalt find from Memory's mere,
> Fount of cool waters flowing clear and free;
> Before which stand the guards, to whom from thee
> Is due this prayer: 'Earth and starry heaven
> Begat me; yet that now to me is given
> Pure heavenly birth, ye know as well as I.
> But I am parched with thirst and like to die;
> Come, give me quick a draught to quench my fear,
> Cool waters flowing free from Memory's mere'.
> That divine stream to quaff they'll grant thee fain,
> Thenceforth with all the heroes thou shalt reign.

Kern, with Eitrem (*Opferritus u. Voropfer*, p. 54), and Dr Jane Harrison
(*Prolegomena to Greek Religion*, p. 594), to refer to the circle of some
sacred dance practised on earth by the priests who initiated the candidate
for Orphic privileges. This suits ποσὶ καρπαλίμοισι excellently; but as
a preliminary and sequel to a re-birth it seems rather puzzling, like so
much else in the magical formulae of all ages.

Fig. 16. Orphic certificate written on gold leaf

The last example,[1] probably from Rome, the second of the two in the British Museum, is much later, belonging to the second century A.D. It was no doubt purchased by or for a noble lady called Caecilia Secundina, whose name indicates that she was, in all probability, a relative of the younger Pliny, Publius Caecilius Secundus as he was called before his adoption by Pliny the Elder. In this case the author of the certificate puts the words into the mouth of some infernal (or supernal) officer at the gate, an Orphic St Peter, who addresses Proserpine, Pluto and Hermes (though the Greek rather suggests that he regarded them all as one), assuring them that he has received the proper passport. He then turns to Caecilia herself and formally admits her, declaring that she has now been born into divine estate. It is brief, and no doubt seemed highly satisfactory to the good lady who purchased it; though one may doubt if she would have been as well satisfied if she had known that it would continue to decorate her mortal remains for 1700 years.

Pure, she comes from the pure, O Queen of the realm of the dead,
Fair daughter of Jove and wise Pluto, and thou by whose hand she was led.
So now there is given me duly this token from memory's pen,
For in song her people remember the life that she lived among men.
Thou hast travelled, Caecilia Scundina, the path that by rule must be trod,
So enter the kingdom rejoicing, new born to the life of a god.[2]

[1] 32 (g) in Kern's *Orphicorum Fragmenta*; see Fig. 16.
[2] Anyone who is at the trouble to compare this version with the Greek will see that the slight expansion it has suffered at my hands is justified by the preceding examples or by the etymology of the Greek names. If Euklees means Pluto and Pluto only, then we have here only two epithets of the same person; but since Hesychius tells us that Eukolos meant Hermes at Metapontum, and since Euklos is distinguished from at least two kinds of Jupiter in the list of Samnite deities found at Agnone (*Italic Dialects*, 175), it is, perhaps, better not to assume that the identity of Euklees and Eubuleus (Pluto) was felt by any but the Orphic authorities. The curious may note with amusement the drastic

The date of this tablet is the most important point. Here we have a cult[1] which has lasted in Italy for over four centuries; a religious cult of a wholly individualistic character having no connexion with any social or political duty, and inculcating with emphasis if not a monotheistic religion, at least what one may call a zeuktotheistic creed. As to the railway porter " cats is dogs and rabbits is dogs ", so to the Orphic believer, Jove and Pluto and Bacchus and Proserpine, Demeter and Cybele and Sarapis, each is as good as the other. We have already seen (p. 22) another source which contributed to this process in Italy.

From these records of Orphic beliefs in Southern Italy it may seem a long step to the sober suggestions of a practical thinker, or even to the imaginative but

suppression of the first vowel of the lady's second name, to meet the requirements of the Hexameter.

[1] For a long time it was held that the spacious and costly buildings of the house known as the Villa Item at Pompeii, more popularly known as the House of the Mysteries, was connected with Orphism; Rostovtzeff, indeed, in the second chapter of his *Mystic Italy* (1927), gave an elaborate interpretation from this point of view of the paintings (or most of them) in the chief room of the villa. The style of the paintings belongs, so he and other archaeologists are agreed, to the period between 80 B.C. and 14 A.D. But although at one or two points in the series of paintings their connection with Dionysus (as a god of fertility) is clear, the nature of the whole series seems to me placed beyond doubt by Miss Jocelyn Toynbee's admirable paper in *J. Rom. Stud.* xix. (1929), p. 67, who has shown that it represents what she rightly describes as "a bride's ordeal", namely, a mystic process of preparing for a happy marriage, in the course of which the rite of flagellation, as it is called, occupied an important part. This curious old-world superstition survived in the practice of the Luperci at Rome, and down to the time of Pausanias at all events, in the flogging of the ἔφηβοι at the altar of Orthia at Sparta (see p. 18, footn.). A German writer, Margarete Bieber, reached very much the same conclusion almost simultaneously (*Jahrb. Deutsch. Archaeol. Inst. Rom.* xliii. pp. 298–330). These interesting pictures, therefore, I leave on one side. The discussion has been continued by Maiuri in his *Villa dei Misteri*, 1930.

finished picture round which a great poet built his national epic. Of Vergil's Apocalypse in the Sixth Book of the *Aeneid* I must not now repeat what I have said elsewhere;[1] but in passing we may note that in spite of Vergil's silence on many points, or rather, indeed, because of it, he presents a more consistent and harmonious conception than any earlier attempt that we possess which can in any way be compared. Its fascinating imagery has exercised no small influence upon subsequent thought, especially in its conception of the life of the Blessed, which, largely through Dante, has become current, if not precisely as a matter of creed, in most forms of Christianity. But it is probable that Vergil himself would have acknowledged his debt[2] to the sober reflections of Cicero, whose brief essay on the After-life was written just when Vergil had completed his own first screed about it in his schoolboy poem, the *Culex*. That poem[3] was written in 54 or 53 B.C.; Cicero's *Dream of Scipio*[4] in the year 54 B.C., and to this we now turn. Cicero followed the example of Plato, who, as many of us remember with delight, concluded his ten Books of the *Republic*, after ranging through a multitude of subjects which no one can call political

[1] *New Studies of a Great Inheritance* (1921), chapter vi ("The Growth of the Underworld").

[2] This is not the place to examine such resemblances as there undoubtedly are between *Aeneid* vi. and the *Somnium Scipionis*, or the question how far they are due to their existence in sources equally familiar to both writers, and how far to Vergil's actual acquaintance with Cicero's work. I must leave this as an interesting topic for study, remarking only that it seems improbable that Vergil, who was wont to read eagerly every book in any kind of study in which he was interested, and who certainly was familiar with Cicero's translation of the Greek astronomer Aratus, drawing upon it frequently in the First Book of his *Georgics*, should not have seized upon the *Somnium*, so closely akin in subject to the poem which in 54 B.C. he had just written.

[3] See *Great Inheritance*, pp. 90 ff.

[4] Cicero, *ad Quint. Fr.* 2. 12 [14]. 1.

(save in the sense that to a philosopher everything is
everything else, or part of it) with a picture of the After-
life, thrown into the form of a long myth told by a
Pamphylian called Er, who came back to life from a
deathlike trance of nine days, and who was obliging
enough to record for the philosopher, and for us through
him, all the wonderful things he had seen in these nine
days while his spirit was wandering far from his body.
Cicero, therefore, taking this for his model, after dis-
cussing the nature and ideals of government in six Books,[1]
concludes by a dream about the After-world which he
attributes to the younger Scipio, that is, to the victor
in the Third Punic War, Scipio Aemilianus (who was the
son of Aemilius Paulus and a Scipio only by adoption).
This young Scipio was a soldier and a statesman; but, like
some other noble minds of his century, he could find no
political party to which he was prepared to attach himself in the fierce dissensions that attended the collapse
of the old Republic, though he was regarded with mingled
respect and fear by both Oligarchs and Revolutionaries.
Cicero represents him as visiting Africa three years before the final destruction of Carthage, and as paying a
visit to the aged African king, Masinissa, who had been
a faithful ally of Rome for more than sixty years. The
conversation of the young Scipio Aemilianus with this
old friend of the house of the Scipios naturally turned on
the deeds of the great Scipio Africanus. Retiring after a
long talk, the king's guest fell into a deep dream in which

[1] A considerable part of these was recovered for us as recently as 1820
by Cardinal Angelo Mai, who found the fragments in the famous palimpsest
in the Vatican underneath a commentary on the Psalms by St Augustine.
But the *Dream of Scipio* had always been known as a part of Book VI,
preserved by Macrobius, luckily for us, since it was not in Mai's fragments.

Scipio Africanus appeared to him and bade him take well to heart what he had come to reveal.

This revelation then, Cicero[1] introduces as a wise man's dream. 'What I have to say about the heavens and about the immortality of the soul', Cicero writes, 'is not the invention of visionary philosophers, or incredible fables such as the school of Epicurus derides; but the conjectures of thoughtful men.'

After a brief prophecy of the future achievements of Aemilianus, including the destruction of Carthage and his second consulship and a hint of the danger to which he would be exposed from civil turmoil, the spirit of the great warrior began to speak on more general themes:

'To encourage you, my grandson, to even greater zeal in defence of our country and its constitution, I would have you know this, that for all those who have saved, served and ennobled their country, there is a place prepared in heaven where they may enjoy blessed and eternal life. For to that divine Author who rules the Universe, nothing that happens on earth is dearer than those unions and assemblies of men linked by the bond of law which are called nations. The rulers and preservers of these unions of men come from Heaven and return thither'.

[The younger Scipio then asked whether he was really to believe that the great Africanus was alive and his own father Paulus also, and others whom men thought of as dead.] 'Yea, verily', answered the great spirit, 'life is theirs indeed who have escaped from the bondage of their bodies as from a prison, whereas what you mortals call life is death. See, there comes your father Paulus to meet you.' When the young Scipio saw his father he shed tears; but Paulus embraced him and forbade him to weep. So then he asked again, 'Tell me, most revered and most kind of fathers, since your existence here is real life, as Africanus tells me, why do I still linger on earth? Why should I not hasten to join you here?' 'Nay,' replied Paulus, 'it is not as you think. For unless that God, who is master of all this sacred region that you see, has set you free from your duty of keeping watch in the body, the gate to this world will not open

---

[1] See *De Re Publica*, 6. § 3.

to you. For human beings have been created under this condition, that they are to keep their watch and station upon that round globe which you see in the centre of this sacred region, that globe called earth. Every one of them has a soul drawn from the eternal fires which you call stars and planets, each of which is a perfect sphere, and quickened by the divine spirit accomplishes with wonderful speed the due orbit of its course. Wherefore, my son, you and every loyal man must keep your soul upon the watch in your body, nor attempt to desert the life of men without commands from Him by whom the soul was given. Beware lest you play the traitor to the duty which God has assigned you. But you, Scipio, following the footsteps of your grandfather here, and mine who begat you, seek after justice and loyalty, of which a great part lies in your behaviour to your parents and kinsmen; but the greatest part of all in your behaviour to your country. So to live is to tread the way that leads to Heaven, and to this assembly, to join those who have left mortal life behind and who, released from the body, now dwell in this region that you see.'

The region that Paulus meant is then explained to be a circuit of glorious light amidst the flaming stars, which the Greeks had taught men to call the Milky Way; and Scipio added that in his vision he saw a number of stars which were never visible on earth and which men had never supposed to exist. Their size far surpassed that of the earth, which indeed seemed to him so small that he was sorry to think that the Empire of Rome could only be called the greatest thing in that globe.

This reflection of the young Scipio's introduces a striking but, for our purpose, hardly relevant description, taken from Greek sources, of the whole system of the nine circles of Heaven, of which the largest and outermost was the very body of God himself, the other seven corresponding to the seven planets and the central being the orb of the earth, round which the rest revolved, and revolved to music; for these seven circles corresponded to the seven notes of the musical scale (poor Mercury and Venus—the planets with the smallest orbits—having to share one note between them). This chapter of pre-Copernican astronomy is followed by an account of the zones of earth and the great super-solar[1] year in which all the planets and stars will have so accomplished their revolutions as at the end of it to return exactly to the point from which they started.

From this Africanus draws a moral of the insignificance of glory among men; for it occupies so small a part of time. The good man must set his eyes on things above and contemplate his celestial abode, his eternal home, not surrendering himself to the desire of popular fame or to the hope of any human rewards, but being attracted to real glory by the beauty of goodness herself. Aemilianus thanked him reverently and promised to strive even more faithfully now that he knew what reward was set before him. To this Africanus replied:

'Yes, strive with all your might and be sure of this, that it is not you that will die, but only your body. For you are not what your mortal shape represents you to be. It is the mind in each man that makes the man, not the bodily form to which others may point. Know, then, that you are a part of what is god, if the word means that spirit which lives strongly and feels and remembers and foresees; which guides and governs and moves the body of which it is to be in charge, no less than God himself guides this Universe of which he is the Author. And as the eternal God himself moves the Universe, which, in part, is subject to decay, so the eternal soul moves our frail bodies'.

Thence, arguing that the nature which is the source of movement must be superior to birth and death, he

[1] Cicero indicates that this Great Year is about 11,000 of our mortal solar years by saying that the period between the death of Romulus and the moment at which he speaks, i.e. roughly 550 years by the Varronian chronology, is not quite a twentieth of the whole.

concludes that the nature of the soul which alone can initiate movement must be immortal.

'This divine spirit of life you must train in noble action, and the noblest of all cares are those which a man maintains for the safety of his fatherland; and if his soul is trained and practised in their pursuit he will all the more swiftly make his way through the heavens to this his everlasting home; and he will do that more speedily if, when he is imprisoned in his body, he still keeps his eyes on what is beyond it, contemplating these things that are beyond, and freeing himself as far as he can from his bodily prison. For the souls of those who surrender themselves to bodily pleasure and make themselves servants to it, and under stress of the desires which it engenders violate their duties to God and man, even when they have made their way out of the body are kept rolling and wallowing like wild beasts round the sphere of earth; and they cannot return to this heavenly region until they have suffered the purification of many ages.' 'With these words he departed, and I', said Aemilianus, 'awoke.'

As compared with the pictures of Orphism and the imaginative setting which Vergil has given them, Cicero's doctrine may seem a little prosaic and unexciting. But this is partly because of the influence it has exerted upon the fathers of the Christian Church, whose teaching, in due course, has left its mark upon our own habits of thought, so that it all sounds rather ordinary; but it has three or four characteristics, some of which correspond to features in Cicero's own conduct of life, and which, taken together, show that his essay marks a growth in the ethical value of the whole doctrine. First of all, there is the deeply felt depreciation of popularity and renown in this world. Cicero had enjoyed this to the full in his consulship; and then, within five years, had learnt that it could not even save him from ignominious banishment. There can be no doubt that this part of the vision inspired one of the most famous declarations of our own poet Milton:

Fame is no plant that grows on mortal soil,
Nor in the glistering foil
Set off to the world, nor in broad rumour lies,
But lives and spreads aloft by those pure eyes
And perfect witness of all-judging Jove;
As he pronounces lastly on each deed,
Of so much fame in Heaven expect thy meed.

Some other points are mainly negative, the things which Cicero preferred to omit. There is no mythology; no great criminals like Tantalus or the more historical Ardiaeus, whom Plato honours by admitting to (apparently) unending punishment. There is none of the picturesque doctrine of migration of souls, a cardinal feature of the Orphic creed, taken over by Pythagoras, and by Plato in his story of the Pamphylian and elsewhere; and then by the Latin poet Ennius, and not quite explicitly rejected by Vergil, although he suggests no other reincarnation than re-birth in human bodies. The limitation is even more marked in Cicero, who speaks of the weaker class of characters as being readmitted to their native heaven only 'after the purification of ages'. It is clearly through deliberate choice that Cicero omits all reference to the nature of this purification, so that the machinery of punishment which occupies a large place in Vergil's picture, and, as we shall see, the largest place of all in the Etruscan doctrine, is nowhere admitted to Cicero's tranquil scene. It is represented by the one word 'purification'. This is typical of the genial and prudent agnosticism which Cicero loved to practise; and it represents also something of the conviction which at this time in his life more and more became paramount in his mind, that force was no remedy for evil.

But these things are, after all, points of detail. The

great difference which we feel in Cicero's attitude towards ethical questions is his steady adherence to the
point of view of public life. Important as that may be,
most of us regard it as only a small part of our conduct.
But we forget the gulf between Cicero's day and our
own. Now we appeal to men to raise their standard of
public conduct to match their private standard, to be
not less honourable, not less generous, not less friendly,
in judging international affairs, than they would be in
their private relations. In Cicero's time the plea was
reversed. If you needed to beg a man to practise any
kind of goodness, what could you appeal to? To his
religion, his reverence for anything connected with it,
or any of its living ministers? It had no bearing whatever upon his morals. Or to any kind of association,
like a church or any other society with a philanthropic
purpose, or even to his political party? None of these
things even existed then. The only society which could
claim from him any moral effort was that of his nation.
To Cicero belongs the distinction—and students of ethics
seem to be agreed that he was historically right[1]—of
placing even the highest rules of private conduct on a
social basis, on the laws inborn in man as a member of
the whole human community. So far as I can find, his
was the earliest recorded declaration[2] in Europe of the

---

[1] See *The Originality of Cicero* (1930), p. 19, footn. 3, reprinted in
a revised form in *Makers of Europe* (Harvard Univ. Press, 1931), p. 36.

[2] *De Leg.* I. § 34, a reference which I owe to a charming address
on the "Humanism of Cicero" by my friend Professor E. K. Rand
(*Proc. Amer. Philos. Soc.* lxxi. 1932, p. 215); the passage must be read,
as Professor Rand reads it, in the light of § 33. What seems to be a
lacuna (and is at all events a corrupt passage) between the two sections,
makes it hard to say how far Cicero meant to extend an attitude which
he puts forward as possible between two like-minded friends; but the

great ideal of conduct based on this natural social tie, an ideal which, as he says, some men held to be impossible, that the wise man should love his fellow no less than himself. And how far Cicero dissented from the severe but heartless morality of the Stoics appears in one point of which I may remind you in conclusion, I mean his clear endorsement of the disapproval which Socrates had felt of suicide. Here Cicero's teaching and conduct was in contrast with the fashionable Stoic doctrine of his day, practised, in fact, by that curious though powerful character Cato of Utica. Cicero more than once[1] seems to make a half-apology in writing to his friends for not having committed suicide rather than go into exile, or rather than submit to Caesar's despotism, and the reasons he gives on both occasions are worthy of his honest and sound humanity. First, because of his children, especially of course his beloved daughter, and, secondly, because of his no less beloved country. And in that spirit, as we know, he faced death when it came.

Let me end with a few words of his[2], which I have quoted before, written, not long before his death, to a trusted friend:

> Do not infer, I beseech you, from these chance jests that I have ceased to care for my country. Believe me, dear friend, day and night my thoughts and endeavours are all set upon this, how to save the lives and the freedom of my countrymen. I let slip no chance of warning, pleading, and planning on their behalf. And my resolve is, that if in thus watching and working I am called to lay down my life, I will count it a glorious ending.

words *hanc benivolentiam late longeque diffusam* suggest that he meant to extend it widely. The second greatest commandment of the Gospels (Mark xii. 28–31, and Luke x. 27–29) is an expansion of Leviticus xix. 18, which dates from the time of the Jewish Exile (W. F. Lofthouse, in *Peake's Commentary*, 1929, p. 196). To this vital question no one but the Good Samaritan gave a final answer.

[1] See *New Studies of a Great Inheritance*, p. 14, and Cic. *ad Fam.* 14. 4. 5 and 9. 18. 2.   [2] *ad Fam.* 9. 24. 4.

CHAPTER III

THE ETRUSCAN INFLUENCE ON ROMAN BELIEFS

HAVING seen something of Orphism and of the cults of two Italian tribes akin in speech, and probably in blood, to the races that were united in what we call Roman stock, we cannot take any step further in tracing the growth of religious sentiment in Ancient Italy without facing at least one side of the most difficult problem in the linguistic history of Europe. I mean the Etruscan question. We certainly know more about the Etruscans now than has ever been known before, but all we know is painfully limited by the difficulty of understanding their language.

We have seen already one feature in the early religions of Italy; many of their gods we have found to represent some definite process of nature or human life in which the worshipper wanted supernatural help.[1] These deities sprang from an attitude of mind practical but apprehensive, and thus ready to be impressed with the warnings and fears common among a set of people with whom the Romans were continually in contact.

The religion of the Etruscans may be described not unjustly as one of fear, and fear to an intense degree; we cannot wonder that it should have left its mark upon the Roman character, especially when we remember that for what seems to have been a period of at least a century

[1] See p. 22.

the public life of Rome was conducted by Etruscan kings; that it was Etruscans who built the triple temple on the Capitol, the most sacred spot in Rome; and that Etruscans had stamped their ideas upon the dress and the pomp of the supreme magistrates, and especially on their behaviour in the crowning ceremony of their career, their return in victory from war; not to mention smaller but rather pervasive details, such as the art of writing and of dividing the year and the month which the Romans owed, partly or mainly, to their Etruscan masters.

Our knowledge of Etruscan religion is derived from many sources; perhaps the most important lies in the direct statements of ancient authorities, especially in the account which Cicero gives us in his interesting discussion of the art and theory of Divination; to which we may add the occasional pictures of Etruscan religious functionaries in poets like Vergil and Ovid. Then we have an avenue of information only recently opened through the study of proper names,[1] which has enabled us to sift out from the mass of recorded Roman names those which show indisputable Etruscan characteristics, such as all the masculine names of the first declension, like *Sulla*, and nearly all that contain the elements -rn-, e.g. *Turnus*, or -nn-, e.g. *Porsenna*, or -ln-, like *Cilnius*. Many of these people took a conspicuous part in Roman history, and their behaviour is instructive.

Finally we have the monuments of the Etruscans themselves, both their articulate writings, of which by slow degrees we are beginning to understand a very little, and

---

[1] See in particular Professor Wilhelm Schulze's *Lateinische Eigennamen*, Berlin, 1904, and my notice of it in the *Classical Review*, xx (1906), p. 411.

their statues and paintings which bear on religious topics. The last class, some of which I will submit in reproductions, is in fact the most eloquent of all.

The two sides of Etruscan religion of which we know most, perhaps indeed they are the only two sides of which there is anything to know, are, first that of Divination and the rites attached thereto; and secondly that of their beliefs about the After-life and the rites attached to them. At the end we shall be able to illustrate from history the effect of these beliefs and practices upon Roman life, and conclude by briefly examining the effect they produced on the mind of one Roman writer who possibly had some Etruscan blood in his veins, but who at all events was exceedingly familiar with the Etruscan religion. And let me say here that if I am to treat the subject before us in any honest way, the evidence I have to bring and interpret may conceivably be unwelcome to some minds unaccustomed to consider the growth of religious ideas; yet they will, I hope, believe me when I say that the historical affinities which I shall suggest, and the view of certain dogmas which the comparison implies, are not offered as an exhaustive treatment, only as a point of view from which, among others, those dogmas must be studied.

The art of divination as the Etruscans conceived it was divided into three branches in which the worshipper, if such he can be called, was instructed what to do about three different things which troubled his mind; namely, first the condition of the entrails, especially the liver, of victims offered for sacrifice; secondly strokes of lightning; and thirdly any other portentous events, including earthquakes. A whole profession of men, known as the

Haruspices (called *netsvis* in Etruscan), were devoted to the 'interpretation' of such phenomena; for a given fee these soothsayers would answer four questions:

(1) By what god the portent was sent.

(2) What offence on the part of the worshipper had caused the portent.

(3) Of what dangers to the worshipper the portent gave warning.

(4) What sacrifices or other proceedings on the part of the worshipper could be relied upon to avert these threatened misfortunes.

This amazing system seems to have been impressed upon the state-religion of Rome by the Etruscan kings, of whom the family of the Tarquins furnished the last. Their tyranny brought to an end the institution of kingship at Rome, which left behind substantial traces of its Etruscan character in more than one side of Roman life, and nowhere more than in religion. To the Etruscan period we must ascribe the institution of the Colleges, as they were called, of Pontiffs and Augurs, who between them, with the help of the *Haruspices*, were responsible for the ritual of public religion. No meeting of the Senate or people could be held, no war could be declared, no battle by sea or land could be begun without the sanction of heaven, which it was the business of the Augur and the soothsayer to seek; and whenever any strange portent was recorded the appropriate ceremonies had first to be dictated by them, and then humbly executed by the highest officers of State with the help of the proper priests.

Most of the doctrine on which these observances were based came from Etruria, though no doubt it embodied some customs used among Italian tribes before the period of Etruscan rule. Of the rules of augury proper, which concerned the flight of various birds, and the ritual which was held to be necessary in order to interpret and to 'expiate'—such was the word they used—to 'expiate' strokes of lightning, and other kinds of portent, I need say nothing now. But the other branch of the art of Divination, that which was based on inspection of the entrails of victims sacrificed to this or that god, is characteristically Etruscan; and it was conducted with such care at Rome that it is worth our attention for a few minutes; especially as we have learnt a good deal about it from recent discoveries.

Here is a picture (Fig. 17, i–iv) of a curious object found at Piacenza in North Italy in 1877.[1] It is made of bronze in a convenient size to be held in the hand, if its round side rests in one's palm. On the flat side are inscribed twice what we know to be the names of a number of Etruscan deities, put into compartments according to the region of the sky which was their respective dwelling-place in the Etruscan theory. An anatomist would smile at the somewhat rudely conventionalised image of the liver of a sheep with its various attachments; but there is no doubt what the image is meant to represent.

The Etruscan words which appear on the flat surface are the names of sixteen different gods, corresponding

---

[1] This photograph and the description is mainly based on Carl Thulin's article on *Die Götter des Martianus Capella* in *Religionsgeschichtliche Versuche* (edited by Dieterich and Wunsch, vol. iii. 1906); but some details come from Thulin's excellent article in Pauly-Wissowa's *Realencyclop.* (vii. 1912), s.v. *Haruspices*; and of course from Cicero's *De Diuinatione* in 43 B.C., and his speech *De Haruspicum Responso* in 57 B.C.

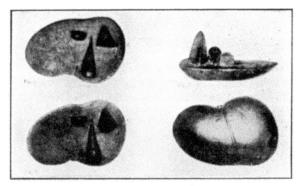

Fig. 17. *Bronze liver of Piacenza*

Fig. 18. *Clay liver from Babylon*

Fig. 19. *The departure of a priest (Corneto tomb)*

to the sixteen divisions which the Etruscans made of the Heavens. These sixteen names are repeated twice over, once round the edge and once in the divisions enclosed inside this ring. Of these names we know the meaning of only seven or eight, of which the chief is Tin which corresponds to the Latin Jove; he appears in three divisions, one for himself, and one for each of two satellites. Among the others mentioned are the Etruscan equivalents of Juno, Mars, Saturn, Liber, Neptune and Silvanus. Any defect in the liver of the victim, at a point corresponding to that marked on this bronze pattern by the name of a particular god, showed, if you please, that he or she must be propitiated by the particular kind of sacrifice which he or she was understood to prefer. And since each god had his own particular way of affecting the worshipper who did not please him, you could count the cost beforehand, if you were so imprudent as to neglect to make the offering prescribed by the priest. The whole liver was divided, as appears, into two halves; that on the right was regarded as the part belonging to you and that on the left the part referring to your enemies. So that a good sign on your enemies' half was as bad for you as an unfavourable sign on the part that related to you. Note in passing the pleasant assumption that every worshipper had enemies to whom he wished evil and who returned his wishes. That the Etruscan religion took for granted, as do so many of the Hebrew psalms.

Now look at the curious projections from the top. The largest, which is of a pyramidal shape, was called 'the head of the liver'. I believe it is now called the *pyramidal process*. This bronze pattern, and another which will appear later, are both, so the anatomists tell us,

copied from a sheep's liver. Anatomists tell us also that
in the sheep the pyramidal projection varies very greatly;
so it made a happy hunting-ground for the priest of this
beautiful faith. If it was very large, that meant good
luck; if it was very small they said it was absent, and that
was terrible; if it was split, that meant a civil war was
impending; if, however, your circumstances were already in a desperate condition, then it was a good thing,
so Pliny tells us,[1] for this queer little pyramid to be split,
because that portended a great change, which might be
for the better.

We learn further from this model and elsewhere[2] that
the gall-bladder was especially connected with Neptune,
and also with Mars, no doubt because it contained liquid,
and was generally red. If it was nearly black it portended
bad luck by sea; if it was especially red you might expect
your house to catch fire. (The muscular streaks, known
as *fibrae*, were also supposed to have a meaning; if they
were especially red, that foretold a drought.[3]) It was a
serious expense to ascertain the will of heaven in this
way, especially if you were not content with the answer
given you by the deity you turned to first. It was a rule
of the priests, who no doubt were on very good terms
with the farmers who bred the cattle, that you could
only find out about one deity by each victim. So you
might go through a whole list of deities with a corresponding number of sheep; and as Cicero[4] asks (no
doubt using an ambiguous phrase on purpose), what are
you to do when Apollo's entrails give you a favourable

1 *Hist. Nat.* 11. 190, *caesum...dirimit curas.*
2 Id. ibid. 11. 195.
3 Fulgentius, *Serm. Ant.* (Helm, p. 112).
4 *de Diu.* 2. § 38.

answer and those of his sister Diana warn you of evil?
Your only obvious duty was to pay the priest for both
victims; but that took you very little further with your
own concerns, except that he probably advised you to
try a third victim.

Before we leave this topic I must submit a similar
monument, now in the British Museum, made of clay
(Fig. 18), which was found on the site of the ancient
Babylon and was dated by Sir Wallis Budge about 2100
B.C. Naturally there are some differences, arising in a
1500 years' interval; yet when we observe the curious
likeness between the two models, especially the importance of the pyramid in both, we shall hardly need
any other evidence to tell us in what region to look for
the origin of the Etruscans.

It seems almost incredible that stuff like this could
have imposed itself upon the credence of a whole nation
for many centuries; but it certainly did. We read, for
instance, that Pompey was greatly addicted[1] to con-
sulting the entrails; and even Julius Caesar carried about
with him a favourite priest, named Spurinna, though he
only attended to his remarks when he thought them
politically convenient. This accomplished Etruscan discovered, so it was said, a few days before the Ides of March
in 44 B.C., that a great bull which was being sacrificed by
Julius Caesar had gone through life without any heart!
Of this Cicero remarked later[2] that the likeliest explanation was that on seeing Caesar in a royal crimson robe
on a golden throne[3] the bull concluded that Caesar must
have lost his head, and so promptly lost his own heart.

[1] Cic. de Diu. 2. § 53.   [2] Cic. de Diu. 2. § 37.
[3] Pliny, Hist. Nat. 11. 186.

(The Latin for a man who has lost his head is *excors*, so that Cicero's jest was immediately intelligible.)

How very serious the political use of the *haruspices* was we may realise best from a single example. When Cicero had been restored from exile in 57 B.C. and his house was given back to him, after having been solemnly confiscated, a process which involved some kind of dedication to the gods, he had to make a long speech to defend his possession; this was because his enemy the infamous Clodius had procured from the *haruspices* a lengthy and oracular declaration that the State was threatened with great evils because it had taken away from the gods what had been pronounced sacred to them. Clodius, we may notice, was hoist with his own petard (a possibility which no doubt the *haruspices* had been clever enough to contemplate); for Cicero was easily able to show that Clodius had committed much greater sacrilege than anything involved in the matter of his own house; and that the dangers to be expected were more likely to come from Clodius than from anyone else. But perhaps the most striking thing in the speech is that Cicero does not dare[1] to impugn the authority of the prediction. Even

---

[1] Examples might be multiplied indefinitely. Augustus and Tiberius set limits to the use of *haruspices*, see for example Dio Cass. 52. 36. 2, and 56. 25; Suet. *Tib.* 63. But Claudius recognised them officially, being proud of his own knowledge of the Etruscan language, see e.g. Tac. *Ann.* 11. 15, 13. 24. The Emperor Alexander Severus actually endowed a professorship in the art of *haruspicina* and provided scholarships for boys who were going to study it; see Hist. Aug. *Al. Sev.* 27. 6, and 44. 4. Constantine and Constantius tried to forbid them; see Cod. Theod. 9. 16. 1 and 4; but Julian made it part of his pagan revival to re-establish them, see Amm. Marc., e.g. 22. 12. 6 and 7. Theodosius abolished it, as we learn from his code, 16. 10. 9 and 12. However, there are other records of them later (e.g. Claudian, *In IV Cons. Hon.* 145), and they were still being prohibited in the seventh century (Mueller-Deecke, *Etrusker*, ii.² p. 18, cite the *decretum Gratiani* of the Concilium Poletanum in A.D. 633).

in his acute analysis of the absurdities of the belief, he is careful to say¹ that it is the duty of a good citizen to follow the customs of his country. Those who would condemn him for this should study a fully documented record of the even more lucrative exploitation of the piety of credulous people, in our own enlightened days, in Dr H. H. Fisher's biography² of the late Mrs Eddy.

Has any epidemic more consuming power than that of superstition?

Turn now to a side of the Etruscan religion in which it took over a set of Greek doctrines which, as we have seen, had once some ethical value. I mean the Orphic-Pythagorean teaching of punishments and rewards in the After-life, paintings of which begin to be frequent in Etruscan tombs of the fourth century B.C. Of these there can be no doubt that the punishments seemed to the Etruscans the more interesting part and the one in which their painters took most delight. There are indeed some scenes of feasting much like what we read of the Mohammedan paradise, but they are comparatively infrequent in the fourth and later centuries B.C.; before that it is difficult to be sure whether the scenes of feasting are anything more than pleasant recollections of what the dead man had enjoyed in his life—indeed he may have had them painted in advance while he was still living. But at all events the doctrine of penalties, when once it had become familiar, was taken up eagerly; and it formed, along with the rules for Divination, all that there was of Etruscan literature. The object of these Acherontic writings, as they were called, we learn from more than one authority;³ it was to provide a kind of *Baedeker's*

¹ See e.g. *de Diu.* 2. §§ 28 and 71.   ² *Our New Religion*, London, 1929.
³ Mart. Cap. 2. 142; Serv. on Aen. iii. 168 and Aen. iii. 231.

Guide to the Infernal Regions, a list of dangers and deities which could be dealt with beforehand, or as one passage suggests[1] even after death, by appropriate sacrifices. By killing certain victims in honour of certain gods at certain seasons, the Etruscan was taught[2] that he could make the soul of a dead man itself into a god, and so deliver it from all the evil powers below.

Figure 19 contains a picture from a tomb[3] at Corneto, the ancient Tarquinii, which shows us the soul of a young priest—so we learn from the inscription (*cesache*)—being marched off to torture by Charu, the tall figure in the background, with the flat nose of a satyr, the pointed ears of an ass, snakes in his forehead, a claw (instead of a right hand) laid upon his victim's shoulder, and the great hammer resting on his own left shoulder. The procession is led by a Fury with a torch with three metal shields. The object of these, it may be conjectured, was to cover a larger portion of the victim's skin with the hot metal than the actual flame of the torch might affect; as the torch burnt down, the largest of these bronze plates would drop off, then the smaller ones would come into play. Another tomb shows a procession of dead souls pursued by devils with hammers or pickaxes, which-ever you like to call them; it may be that Dante owed his notion[4] of the devils with rakes (*roncigli*) to this tradition. He may even have seen that very picture.

Figure 20 is a sketch given by Brun[5] from the Tomba

[1] Mart. Cap. 2. 140; see p. 63, footn. 1.   [2] Arnob. 2. 62.
[3] The Tomba del Tifone; cf. Fr. Poulsen, *Etruscan Tomb-painting* (1922), p. 58.
[4] *Inferno*, Canto xxi and xxii. For his familiarity with Corneto, see Canto xiii. 9, a passage cited by Weege, *Etruskische Malerei* (Halle, 1921), p. 48.
[5] *Ann. Ist. Arch.* 1866, p. 422.

Fig. 20. *The departure of Anes Arnth (Bruschi tomb)*

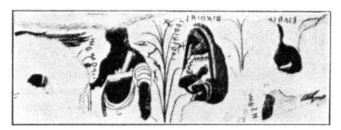

Fig. 21. *Teiresias and Memnon in hell*

Fig. 22. Hades, Persephone and Geryon

Bruschi at Corneto; it shows a young man named *Anes Arnth Velthur* saying good-bye to his father and being carried off by devils.

We possess also several eighteenth-century sketches of paintings from Corneto which have since fallen to pieces. The pictures[1] show us souls suspended to receive punishment, *suspensae ad uentos*, as Vergil calls it, and their torturers are advancing upon them with a hammer and a burning torch, and a curious implement intended to tear the skin from their bodies, perhaps what Plautus calls *inductores* when used upon slaves ('persuaders' or perhaps 'plasterers').

The next (Fig. 21) is still in existence in a tomb at Corneto. Between the shades of Teiresias and Memnon[2] is an asphodel plant with little souls hung on to it by any one of their limbs—head, feet, arms and the rest. And that these grim imaginations correspond to things that were actually done to unfortunate slaves we have sadly plentiful evidence.[3] Next we have some remarkably faithful[4] restorations, which you may see in the Etruscan Museum at Florence, of figures from the underworld. The first (Fig. 22) shows us Hades and Persephone enthroned in the cloudy inferno; notice their headdress and the snake which Hades carries in his left hand, and

[1] Given by Weege, *Etr. Malerei*, p. 33, from Dempster's *De Etruria Regali* (1724).

[2] In Etruscan *teriasals* and *memrun*.

[3] E.g. Plaut. *Asin.* 301, 549 (*inductoresque acerrumos gnarosque nostri tergi*); *Capt.* 998.

[4] Their truthfulness appears from comparing them even with the colourless photographs of what still actually remains in the tombs, given, e.g. by Weege, *Etr. Malerei*, to whose learning I am much indebted. For the photographs from Florence, I am indebted to the kindness of the Director of the Museum, Professor A. Minto, and of my friend Mr J. A. Spranger.

the three-headed giant Geryon who is receiving instructions.

Figure 23 shows us the same infernal pair watching a feast being prepared.

The next (Fig. 24) is from Florence again; the raven type of devil is a particularly favourite image in these paintings; his name was *Tuchulcha*. Besides his beak and his snaky head he carries snakes and either a torch or a hammer, and he is torturing Theseus. This comes from the Tomba dell' Orco at Corneto.

We have seen enough by this time to realise that it was not a pleasant thing in Etruria to fall into the hands of Death. Admirers of the Etruscans[1] have apologised for the brutality of these pictures by pointing out that these scenes from the underworld do not appear in Etruria before the fourth century B.C., and that the general doctrine of purification by punishment after death was not invented in Etruria, but came thither from sources which may be called either Orphic[2] or Pythagorean. But how did the Etruscans apply this belief in practice?

The trembling Etruscan had no great confidence in mere initiation which satisfied many Greek minds; he could only be saved, if saved at all, by a long process of sacrifices and offerings conducted by the priestly profession, which was a wealthy and influential part of every Etruscan community—a process, too, which needed to be continued after the man's death. That at least is suggested by a passage in Martianus Capella, where the heroine re-

---

[1] Weege, *Etr. Malerei*, p. 23; Randall-MacIver, *The Etruscans*, pp. 52 and 128.

[2] See the preceding chapter.

Fig. 23. *Hades and Persephone before a feast*

Fig. 24. *Tuchulcha torturing Theseus (Corneto)*

joices to have been rendered immortal by a magical potion without descending to the Lower World;[1] and seems to be confirmed (though no one can say this is yet certain) by the character of the longest Etruscan document which we possess.

At the beginning of the present century there was observed upon the linen wrappings of an Egyptian mummy, in the Museum at Agram in Austria, a quantity of ancient writings which proved to be in the Etruscan language; and from the character of the ink and other external features it seems to have been written not long before the Christian era, by some Etruscan settlers in Egypt. If we were even yet able to translate any continuous portion of this book I should have liked to dwell upon it, for its possibilities are full of interest. As it is, I must content myself with saying that most of the small number of people who can be called Etruscan scholars believe, mainly from the fact that it contains the names of a number of deities, and was wrapped round a mummy, that it is a copy of the Liturgy used by the Etruscans for procuring the deliverance of a dead person from the penalties which we have seen pictured on their tombs.

The doctrine of Purgatory as a process of purification we have seen to be of Orphic origin; that is, it came from somewhere in the East or perhaps simply from Egypt,[2] and was known to the Greeks not later than the

[1] Mart. Cap. (2. § 140 ff.) gives details of her rejoicing thus: 'Because she had not been obliged to set eyes upon the god of the Underworld with his wife, as the Etruscans used to ordain; nor to tremble at the Furies or the Chaldean horrors; nor to submit to burning by fire or purification by water...; nor to seal her immortality, a gift wrapped in the snaky hands of Charon, by suffering death herself first'.

[2] E. A. Wallis Budge, *The Book of the Dead*, London, 1929, iii. p. 10. "The Papyros of Nesi-Khensu...is...the copy of a contract which is

sixth century B.C. The first trace of its adoption by Christian communities is in writings of teachers like Clement of Alexandria and Tertullian,[1] in the third century A.D. But in all these passages there is no hint that fees paid by relatives after a man's death, or by himself before death or through his will, will have any effect upon his subsequent career.

The view taken by the noblest minds of the Catholic faith in the Middle Ages is finely illustrated by the reply given to Dante[2] by Vergil when he wonders why the souls in Purgatory should beg him to pray for them:

'Because the burning flame of love can complete in one moment all the satisfaction that should be rendered by the soul in Purgatory'.

In Dante's mind it is not the mere saying of prayers that can do the miracle, but the intense fire of love, of

declared to have been made between Nesi-Khensu and Āmen-Rā, 'the holy god, the lord of all the gods'. As a reward for the great piety of the queen, and her devotion to the interests of Āmen-Rā upon earth, the god undertakes to make her a goddess in his kingdom, to provide her with an estate there in perpetuity and a never-failing supply of offerings, and happiness of heart, soul and body, and the [daily] recital upon earth of the 'Seventy Songs of Rā' for the benefit of her soul in the Khert-Neter, or Underworld. The contract was drawn up in a series of paragraphs in legal phraseology by the priests of Āmen, who believed they had the power of making their god do as they pleased when they pleased."

[1] Clement of Alexandria (*Strom.* 6. 6) says that 'God's punishments in Hades are saving and disciplinary, leading souls to conversion'. Tertullian (*de Carnis Resurr.* 43) in commenting on II Corinthians v. 8 says: 'for no one who becomes absent from his body is immediately at home with the Lord, except by the prerogative of the martyrs, who are destined to stay in Paradise and not in the Lower World'. In *De Anima* (55–58) he expounds the same doctrine, that Martyrs go straight to Heaven, but that the rest of men wait in the Lower World for the day of the Lord (*sequestrari apud inferos in diem Domini*), undergoing such courses of punishment as will free them from sin.

[2] *Purg.* vi. 38f.:

> Perchè fuoco d'amor compia in un punto
> Ciò che dee soddisfar chi qui s'astalla.

which prayer may be the symbol. But the form in which
we find it among the Etruscans, as in the papyrus[1] of Nesi-
Khensu, is the payment of fees to professional men whom
you believe to be capable of working the miracle for you.
And it is difficult to doubt that there is an historical connexion between this and the similar usage in the Roman
Catholic Church to-day—at least if I am rightly informed
that Masses for the Dead are recited on the payment of
fees or in return for a gift to the Church before death
or by Will. In any case, it is certainly true to describe
the practice as being intrinsically Etruscan, and Egyptian.
It was spread over a great part of Italy under Etruscan
influence long before Christ was born; but it has been
carried by the priests of the Roman form of Christianity
as part of their professional and financial apparatus all over
this long-suffering world.

It is a commonplace of historians that intense superstition, especially superstition linked with fear, is linked
also with cruelty; and this is a feature in the Etruscan
character, which, though it found congenial expression
in depicting the torments of the dead, was far older than
the arrival of the Orphic doctrines in the fourth century
B.C.; and far younger too, as you will remind me, if you
know Dante's picture of the torturing devils in the Inferno, some of whose implements, as we have seen,[2]
seem to have been directly suggested to him by the pic-

[1] See p. 63, footn. 2.
[2] See above, p. 60. The most horrible of all the tortures which Dante
conceived is the perpetual devouring of the head of a murderer by his
victim, Canto xxx. 1 and xxxiii. 76; and this seems to have been suggested
by a misunderstanding, though a misunderstanding in form rather than
in spirit, of the picture of Pluto wearing a helmet consisting of a wolf's
head showing the teeth, and eyes that seem still alive and flashing with
malevolence.

tures at Corneto. The truth is that this side of Dante betrays his Tuscan blood. On this side he is the genuine descendant of the people who stoned to death in the market-place of Caere all the Phocaean captives whom they had taken at the naval battle of Alalia in the sixth century B.C.; and who in 358 B.C. put to death by sacrifice in cold blood, at Tarquinii, a body of 307 Roman captives. The Roman Dictator Sulla followed the Etruscan tradition, which his name[1] implies, by slaughtering six thousand Samnite captives in Rome in the hearing of the Senate in 83 B.C.

And there are other figures in Roman history who bear the same mark of Etruscan origin as Sulla, namely, a masculine name ending in -a, Ahala, Cinna, Perperna, Catilina, Casca, all known for their bloody deeds; Sisenna was the zealous supporter of the monster Verres. Others, like Caecina and Ofella, are known for acts of treachery. Add to these Mamurra, the luxurious and fraudulent bankrupt, the *decoctor Formianus* whom Catullus attacks.

There is one, and only one on the list, the Emperor Nerva, who can be named as a man of noble character. One other Etruscan, Maecenas, served Rome well at a crisis by his brilliant gifts of diplomacy and his faithful friendship to Vergil, which included the capacity of adopting Vergil's thoughts and impressing them upon Augustus. His private life, however, was typically Etruscan.

But it is not merely isolated individuals in whom this racial characteristic appears; it is well known to all students of Etruscan art that the subjects which the Etruscans chose from the Greek legends for decorative purposes in paintings, or vases, or to be chased on the backs of silver

[1] See p. 51 and W. Schulze, *Lat. Eigennamen*, p. 417.

Fig. 25. *Sacrifice of Trojan captives by Achilles (François tomb)*

Fig. 26. *Etruscan sports*

mirrors, or beautifully engraved on the precious stones set in rings or used for seals, were most frequently of a tragical kind, especially scenes of slaughter. Let me give you one instance only (Fig. 25) from the so-called François tomb at Vulci. It represents[1] the slaughter of two Trojan captives by Achilles at the tomb of his friend Patroclus; one of the Trojans, whose hands are bound behind him, is seated, and Achilles is in the act of driving his sword into his throat. The painter has been at pains to represent the splashes of blood; the next victim stands with his hands bound, looking on with horror and awaiting his turn, guarded by the warrior Ajax. The ghost of Patroclus is looking on at the vengeance and so is Agamemnon, and two characteristic Death-Gods of the Etruscans, Vanth with the black wings, and Charu with his hammer. In the Etruscan section of Furtwängler's splendid collection[2] of ancient gems, a considerable number represent scenes of human sacrifice; one of them pictures the dismemberment of a small child.

Perhaps you will defend this by saying that these scenes are dramatic and might attract the imagination of a serious artist; take now one other picture (Fig. 26) of a different kind representing a scene of sport. You will wonder what is happening; and so far as I know that particular kind of sport is not recorded of anyone but the Etruscans. In the scene on the right,[3] one of two rivals has his legs entangled in a lasso which the other has thrown, and his

[1] Reproduced by Poulsen, *Etruscan Tomb-painting*, p. 12; the next he gives on p. 54, from the Tomba degli Auguri at Corneto.

[2] *Antike Gemmen*, Berlin, 1900, p. 229. Dennis, *Cities and Cemeteries of Etruria*, Ed. 2 (1878), ii. p. 92, gives a long list of murderous scenes from Etruscan vases.

[3] The other scenes of wrestling, and archery, with two umpires and an onlooker, do not concern us here.

head is covered by a sack with which the other has managed to blindfold him; and while he is at this disadvantage, he is being attacked by a bloodhound, who has already inflicted on him two serious wounds from which the blood is streaming. In a companion picture, not included in these photographs, which apparently represents an earlier part of the contest, the man with the dog and the lasso is running away; he has no other weapons; but by some clever turn he caught his opponent, with the results we have just seen. You will say perhaps that that is not so desperate a sport as the fighting of gladiators with which we are familiar in Rome. Perhaps not, but where did the gladiators come from? They were first introduced into Rome at the funeral of a man of Etruscan blood and Etruscan name, D. Junius Pera, in the year 264 B.C.; such combats at funerals had long been in use in Etruria, as we know from many pictures in Etruscan tombs. And the habit of putting to death prisoners of war, if possible as a public show, was permanently represented in Rome at the end of every triumphal procession, an institution which we know in all its details to have been introduced by the Etruscan kings. As soon as the procession reached the foot of the Capitol, those prisoners of war who had been reserved to grace the victorious general's triumph, and had marched in the procession before him in his chariot, were led aside[1] and put to death in cold blood; the whole procession paused while this was done.

The Etruscanised deities who presided over the temples of the Capitol would not receive the thanks of the triumphant general until their ears had been filled with the

[1] See among other authorities Cic. *II Verr.* 5. § 30.

Fig. 27. The Apollo of Veii

sweet sounds of death by the sword. The Etruscan, no less than the dark rulers of Dahomey before the advent of British rule, was convinced that freshly shed blood brought joy to the spirit of the dead. These bloody customs lasted on in Rome, in spite of the disapproval of humaner spirits like Cicero and Vergil, until four centuries later the gladiatorial shows were suppressed by Christian protest. "Tantum potuit suadere malorum" religio Etrusca, drawn like the rest of their mentality from the lower stratum of the eastern world.

There is one of the monuments of Etruscan art which seems to illustrate almost better than anything else their prevailing temper. It is the famous statue of Apollo at Veii (Fig. 27). I need hardly remind you that to the Greeks the name of Apollo meant everything that was wise, enlightened and humane—music, medicine, art, and poetry. Nor need I stop to illustrate this from the many beautiful representations of this god which the Greeks have left to us. The Etruscan statue was found in 1916 in the ruins of Veii and belongs (so archaeologists tell us) to 520 or 510 B.C., long before the Orphic doctrines had spread in Etruria.

It is described thus by Dr Randall-MacIver, who will not be suspected of any prejudice against the Etruscans, and who prefixes it to his lucid account of them[1]: "I would say that this is the most perfect incarnation of an entirely remorseless, inhuman god that can be imagined; the severity, the ruthlessness, the terrifying beauty haunt the memory". What Dr MacIver calls "beauty", I confess I should rather describe as a vulgar leer, though the details of drapery and flesh are beautifully executed. The

[1] *The Etruscans*, Oxford, 1927.

whole figure shows what became of Greek ideas when they were transferred to Etruscan minds.

Nothing can remove the stain of cruelty from the character of the ancient Etruscan; yet he was after all a human being, and it will perhaps leave behind a fairer conception of what a real Etruscan was like if we end by recalling one of the most splendid of the pictures in Vergil's Gallery of Warriors, that of the Etruscan tyrant Mezentius.

Let us first observe that Vergil knew a great deal about the Etruscans, not merely because of his study of the different sides of life in all ancient Italy, but especially because he was a native of Mantua, a city which was Etruscan in foundation and whose chief families, as he himself tells[1] us, were of Etruscan blood. And of the great Etruscan profession of soothsayer Vergil had definite opinions; he had seen not merely their fallibility (Rhamnes, Aen. ix. 327–328), but their presumptuous interference in grave matters (Tolumnius, xi. 429; xii. 258 and 461), and their treachery (Calchas, ii. 123–125). In the *Georgics* (ii. 193) he describes the choicest kind of wine as that in use at sacrifices, 'when the fat Etruscan has blown his ivory trumpet at the altar', playing the trumpet and the tibia in public being arts reserved for Etruscans.[2] And in the tenth Book of the *Aeneid*, the only one in which there is any approach to the brutality of speech regular between the warriors in Homer, there is only one example[3] of coarse personal invective, and it is put into the mouth of Tarchon, the Etruscan com-

[1] *Aen.* x. 203.

[2] See the amusing story of the strike of the Etruscan *tibicines*, in Livy, 10. 30; and Ovid, *Fast.* 6. 53 ff.

[3] *Aen.* xi. 732–740.

mander, who, in order to rouse his troops from their cowardice, reviles their private characters quite in the style of Achilles, when he addresses[1] Agamemnon as 'drunken, dog-eyed devourer of the people'.

In Mezentius we have Vergil's study of an Etruscan king. We hear of him first from the lips of Evander, his civilised neighbour of Greek birth, who tells Aeneas why Mezentius has been cast out by his subjects and has fled with his son and a few followers for refuge to his friend Turnus, the Rutulian prince. Mezentius had been guilty of shameful murders and other tyrannical acts in his stronghold of Caere; among them the practice of killing his victims by a peculiar form of torture, of which I seem to have read when I was younger as being still in use by a certain race in Eastern Europe. Mezentius bound his living victim tightly, face to face to a corpse, and left him to die of starvation and the horrible embrace.[2]

But when Mezentius appears on the battle-field, we realise that if he has the cruelty or more than the cruelty of a beast, he has also the courage. He is compared to a wild boar at bay and to a hungry lion who has just slain a stag, his jaws still wet with its blood. All his speeches are brutal and impious; while other warriors pray to their favourite god to help them, he prays to his own right hand, and vows his own son to be the trophy of his victory,[3] clothed in the spoil that he hopes to take from

[1] Iliad, i. 225ff.

[2] This Etruscan practice, as used upon the hapless sailors whom their pirate vessels had captured, is further attested by Aristotle (Fr. 60, Rose, p. 71) quoted by Cicero (*Hortens.* Fragm. 88, Baiter).

[3] *Tropaeum Aeneae*, 'a sign of the defeat of Aeneas'; but since the word is more often used with the genitive of the person who erects the trophy (e.g. Hor. *Odes*, 2. 9. 19), I am inclined to wonder whether Vergil did not mean the words to be ambiguous, and so suggest a bad omen.

the body of his enemy, the pirate Aeneas. In their en-
counter, the spear of Aeneas pierces his shield and wounds
him in the thigh, but he is saved by his brave young son
Lausus, who dashes in upon Aeneas and thus gives his
father time to retreat; the followers of Lausus rush up,
and for the moment Aeneas is hard pressed, though they
cannot pierce his defence. He warns Lausus not to persist
and offers to let him go free, with words of admiration
for the dutiful courage which the young prince has shown,
but Lausus refuses and rushes upon his doom. Aeneas
stays the fighting and with words of pity lifts the boy's
body from the ground and with his own hands surrenders
it for burial to his followers. Meanwhile Mezentius is
resting at a distance, with his great horse Rhaebus beside
him, until at length he receives[1] the news of his son's
death. How does he greet it?

> 'Did such besetting love of life, my son,
> Possess me that I let the foe's right hand
> With all its weight fall upon thee, on thee?
> Have thy wounds saved me? By thy death live I
> Thy father? Never knew I till this hour
> The smart of exile; now the curse comes home,
> Now the wound pierces deep. And none but I,
> None but thy sire, o son, has shamed thy name,
> Driven by a people's hatred from the throne
> And sceptre of my fathers. I alone
> Owed expiation to my fatherland;
> Sword, fire or torture should have first annealed
> This guilty spirit. Yet do I survive?
> Have I not yet quit light and humankind?
> But I shall quit them.' And with that he rose
> Upon his stricken knee; and though the pain
> Of that deep wound oppressed him, undismayed
> He bade them bring his horse, his pride of old,

[1] Aen. x. 846.

His trusty comrade who had brought him home
Victor from all his warfare, and who now
Gazed sadly on his lord. Then spake the king:
    'Too long, my horse, if ought that's long there be,
For creatures born to perish, we have lived.
Either to-day thou shalt have yonder arms,
Stained with Aeneas' blood, crowned with his head,
And so avenge the slaughter of my son,
Or, if no might of ours can force a way
To reach that triumph, die with me thy master.
For ne'er, brave steed, I know, wilt thou endure
The voice of strangers or a Trojan lord'.

Then he rides to the last conflict, in which Aeneas hurls his spear full into the forehead of the horse, who falls to the ground, leaving his master defenceless. Mezentius welcomes death, begging only that his body be buried so that his own people may not wreak their vengeance upon it.

In two things Mezentius wins our admiration: his undaunted courage, and the affection he has for his son and his horse. He has nothing of what we call religion: as he says, he 'stays for no god's bidding'. And yet he shares with his countrymen one kind of belief, just that which we have seen so fully depicted in their tombs, the belief in some power that rejoices to inflict the cruellest punishment; and that is why he owns his defeat. The death of his son brings him to confess his own ill-deeds. That conception of the deity as being above all a lover of vengeance and human blood, we know well in other races of the East, Jehovah in Abram's first conception of him, Juggernaut, Baal, Moloch and the rest. And it is the grim distinction of the Etruscans to have brought it with them to Italy and to have stamped it deeply upon the imagination of the people of Rome, and upon the form of Christianity which Rome was to convey to the world; so deeply that in what is known as the Forensic theory of the Atonement it has exerted, and has not yet ceased to exert, what thoughtful students[1] of Christian doctrine have long felt to be a barbarising influence in the Protestant as well as in the Roman Church.

[1] Such as Macleod Campbell (*Nature of the Atonement*, 1886) and Horace Bushnell (*Vicarious Sacrifice*, 1891). More generally see the interesting history of this conception in Christian writers by W. Adams Brown in Hastings' *Encyclopaedia of Religion and Ethics* (vol. v. 1912). To this, if a layman in theology may venture to add anything from his private reading, I cannot but feel that the brilliant analysis of the nature of Forgiveness and its application to Christian history which was given by Dr Edwin Abbott Abbott (in chapters xiii and xvi of *Through Nature to Christ*, London, 1877) provides an important completion. Abbott's view, while it resembles those of Macleod Campbell and Bushnell in excluding all associations of the Penal theory and insists upon the regenerative power of sympathetic forgiveness, does not exclude the element of vicarious suffering, since that is implied in all true sympathy. This was pointed out to me some forty years ago by my friend the Rev. W. S. Houghton, of Edgbaston. And it is worth while to record what I learnt from Dr Abbott's own lips, that the central incident in the story of Daniel Deronda was devised by George Eliot in response to a suggestion made to her by him that she should write a story to illustrate the power of human forgiveness. Soon after the book appeared, she said to him at one of her receptions, "You see I have carried out your suggestion".

CHAPTER IV

BREAKING THROUGH THE MAZE

In the summers of 1930 and 1931 it was my good fortune, thanks to the enterprise of a body of American
scholars and teachers, to accompany them in visiting
all the great seats of Greek religion (following the travels
of Vergil so far as we know them, and the course of his
hero Aeneas) around the coasts and islands of Ancient
Hellas—Athens, Eleusis, Delos, Delphi and Olympia,
not to speak of such centres of ancient life as Mycenae,
Crete and the Hellespont, as well as the site of Troy;
and finally the Greek, or half-Greek remains in the west,
such as Syracuse, Taormina, Pesto and Cumae. To see
all these was to receive more than one deep impression
of the character of the religion whose relations with the
life of Italy and whose effect thereby upon the life of
Europe we are briefly to examine now. Two feelings in
particular fill my mind in the recollection. The first,
of the large and cheerful part in the daily life of the
Greeks which was made by the great temples and the
ceremonies and processions of which these temples were
the centre; and, secondly, of the multitude of picturesque
and generally romantic stories with which these holy
places were connected—Athens, besides its splendid record in history, recalling picturesque legends like that
of the competition between Poseidon and Athena for the
worship of its citizens, in which Poseidon produced the
horse by a blow on the earth with his trident but Athena

carried the day with her gift of the olive-tree, the pride of every Attic farm; Eleusis, with its pathetic story of the wanderings of Demeter in search of her stolen child, and the great Mysteries which offered, to the privileged few, strange hopes of life after death; Delphi, in front of stupendous cliffs and glistering waterfalls, looking out across the forest of grey olives and the blue waters of the Corinthian gulf to the mountains of the Peloponnese, far removed in what seems, and was, a different world; Delphi, the scene of a score of myths in which the divine and beautiful Apollo had played a very human part; Delos, that silvery coronet of rock rising gently from a sapphire sea, its few acres crowded with the marble columns of a hundred temples, bearing witness to the piety of all the cities that sent their crews of mariners past its dangerous coast, with its pretty tale of the birth of Leto's two fair children, Apollo and Artemis, in spite of the designs of their enemy; and Crete, Mycenae, Troy and Olympia, with their long stories, half myth, half history, of colossal wealth, of love and treachery and murder and war after war.

These two feelings, of the splendour and the romance of these Greek sites, were inevitably linked with a third, forced upon one by every book written in the great period of Roman literature, the last century B.C., a lively sense of the gulf between the way in which these sides of religion were at that date regarded by the thoughtful and educated Roman on the one hand, and on the other by the Italian peasants and the common folk of the towns.

We must start from the most obvious feature of the old Italian religion or religions, which is really implied in what we have already seen, namely the enormous

number of deities which sprang from the Italian habit of
attaching some divine entity to every important process
of nature or human life. What was the situation in this
field of men's psychology when we come down to this
age, say from 70 to 20 B.C.? It is difficult to get any
phrase loose enough to describe the chaos of ideas which
the period presents.

Among all the gods of the nations, those of early
Italy, as we have seen,[1] have a character of their own, a
character which we can call dull and interesting with
equal justice. They are dull because they (or at least
most of them) are not persons in any real sense. They
are interesting because, as in the case of *Tursa* at Iguvium,
they represent definite proceedings in which the worshipper desired supernatural help.

He turned to his *Penates* to keep his *penus* (i.e. his
larder) stocked, to *Ceres* to make his cornfield flourish,
to *Silvanus* to make his trees grow, to *Faunus* to make
his sheep bear lambs; *Lupercus* would keep the wolves
away; *Flora* brightened his garden; *Terminus* prevented
his neighbours from trespassing on his fields; *Robigus*
must be propitiated lest he should inflict red rust on the
wheat; he must trust *Portunus* to look after his harbours,
and *Fortuna* to do what she could for him with things
that came by chance. Of just the same sort were the
deities of which we so frequently hear in Rome, where
there were temples to 'Prudence', 'Valour', 'Victory',
'Good Health' and 'Good Faith'; and these are the
deities which Plautus makes fun of with his 'Cleanli-
ness',[2] 'Food-stuffing',[3] 'Jesting', 'Sport', 'Conversation' and 'Sweet-kissing',[4] and others.

[1] P. 22.   [2] Cas. 225, *Munditia*.   [3] Capt. 877, *sancta Saturitas*.
[4] Bacch. 116, *Iocus, Ludus, Sermo, Suauisuauiatio*.

The list might be greatly prolonged, and so far were they from having a personal character that the sex of some of them, like *Pales*, god of pasturing sheep, and even in the old days, *Venus*, was undetermined, and grammarians gravely discussed whether they ought to have a masculine or feminine adjective—hence the pious formula preserved for us in many examples of prayers, *seu deus, seu dea es*, 'whether you are a god or a goddess'. From the form of the word it is clear that *Venus* was, to start with, exactly what (I am told) is understood in cinematographic society by the neuter pronoun *It*, namely an abstract noun, meaning 'charm' or 'desire', of the same type as *genus* or *onus*. So *Ceres*, probably, to start with, meant merely 'growing', 'germinating', and possibly *Pales* meant merely 'grazing' or 'pasture'.

Now on the top of this extensive and rather costly, but very intangible, swarm of gods, a new world of ideas and stories was imposed through a period of centuries, by many different channels; from above and below, by the instructions and public acts of the government, by oracles, Sibylline and other, by Greek comedies on the stage, by friendly Greek neighbours and tutors, and by a multitude of foreign slaves under one's own roof. In the light of this new and attractive mythology, poor Ceres could no longer attend to her own business of making the corn grow, without being mixed up in the misfortunes of Proserpina, merely because the Greek goddess Demeter ('Mother Earth') had once lost her daughter Persephone to the king of the dark Underworld, who carried her off from the flowery fields of Enna in Sicily; and her mother's grief constrained the higher powers to liberate her for six months in the year from his gloomy realm, and give her back to life above ground every year with the spring flowers, until the autumn came and sent her down again. The old Italian god Liber could no longer look after the vines and the wine made from them without having to take on the responsibilities for more than one type of drama, for literature, and even for the routs and orgies in honour of intoxication that different tribes of Greeks and Phrygians and Thracians had attached to Bacchus.

The result of this mixture of ideas, as we know, was that, on the one hand, the Romans saw no limit to the number of gods, and were always prepared to be interested in, or to worship, a new one who seemed likely to be useful; and, on the other hand, great uncertainty, even among the most orthodox kind of people, about the truth of the stories with which they came to be familiar by inheritance or otherwise. The process had gone on for a long time till all the reading public, and, indeed, every schoolboy, was familiar with a large number of Greek myths; so that it was of no use to tell anyone that *Jove*, for example, was a youngster, or that *Diana* had any interest in cookery, or that *Hercules* was a patron of the fine arts.

But the more thoughtful minds of Rome who knew their way about Greek literature did not confine themselves to its poets. They read, and read deeply, of its philosophy, and more than read; for the most distinguished living Greek philosophers loved to go and lecture in Rome (and had done for more than a century); and the critical and sceptical spirit, which, from the time of Socrates and before him, the Greeks had applied to their own mythology, produced an even deeper impression on the best minds than had the stories which the philosophers demolished. Epicurus in particular, whatever may be said about him as a philosopher or man of science, had been highly successful in his matter-of-fact way of exploding the old-world legends associated with the names of the Greek gods. His pupil Lucretius, who was also largely his translator, brought to the same task the high and serious mind of the uncorrupt section of the Roman nobility, united with the enthusiasm of the poet and moral reformer. Let me illustrate this by a rendering of the well-known passage[1] in which Lucretius tells, with mingled scorn and pity, the story of Agamemnon's sacrifice of his own daughter at the bidding of the soothsayer Calchas, in order to secure favourable winds to carry the Greek fleet from Aulis to Troy—one of the most famous stories, no doubt in some sense historical, connected with the Trojan War. The name by which Lucretius knew the victim was *Iphianassa*.

> 'Oft has Religion fathered impious deeds;
> Even as, at Aulis, Iphianassa's blood
> Darkened Diana's altar, foully shed
> By all the prime of Grecian chivalry.
> When the white wreath of sacrifice, impressed
> On girlish tresses, hung beside her cheeks,
> And when she marked her father's mournful face
> Beside the altar, and his serving-men
> Hiding a sword, and all the gazing crowd
> Weeping to see her, dumb in fear she knelt
> Beseeching. But it naught availed her then
> That long ago her lips first called him 'father'.
> Seized by rude hands and trembling she was led
> Before the altar, not to be a bride
> And hear the pomp of ancient ceremonies
> Crowned with the loud rejoicing nuptial song,

[1] I. 82–100.

But in the maiden blossom of her years
To fall like some poor sheep in sacrifice
Struck by her father's hand; that so the fleet
With fair and holy auguries might be sped.'

The conclusion drawn by Lucretius was, as we all know, that every kind of religious belief was equally false, that men were merely machines, controlled by the fortuitous concourse of ever-moving atoms, into which they were again resolved completely after death. The gods, whose existence he did not in name deny, had nothing whatever to do with the course of the world or of human life, which was governed by fixed physical laws.

But the ethical doctrine of Epicurus, that pleasure was the end of life, was repugnant to every Roman instinct, and it was not upon these lines that the main stream of Roman thought and conduct was destined to run. It was the rival school of Stoics, with their rigid ideal of virtue and the service of the community, which every other Latin writer whose work has come down to us, save the clever but worthless Sallust, did in fact profess, though with reservations in practice. But this did not repair the breach which Greek criticism had made, for the Stoics were no more ready than the Epicureans to accept Greek myths at their face value; yet they did believe very strongly in one central, providential Power, which governed the Universe. Cicero represents for us the better part of Stoicism, though he makes fun of the entanglements of their severely verbal logic. Of the feeling of the best Romans at the end of the Republic we need seek in prose no more dignified expression than Cicero's conclusion of his whole discussion of the so-called Art of Divination, which, as we saw in a previous essay, the Etruscans had imposed on the public life of Rome. This[1] is what Cicero writes:

> ' We must then surely dismiss with abhorrence divination drawn from dreams as well as all the other kinds; for, if we may speak frankly, it is a superstition which has spread over many nations, taking captive the popular mind and the common weakness of humanity. That has been my chief hope in this discussion; I felt that I should have rendered no small service to myself, and to any whom I could influence, if I could destroy this superstition root and branch. And yet (this I am anxious to make clear) religion is not abolished by our abolishing superstition. The wise man will maintain the customs of his ancestors by due observance of sacred rites and ceremonies; and that there is some transcendent and eternal Nature, and one to which the race of men ought to look with reverence, is a fact which the wise man must acknowledge if he considers the beauty of the universe and the whole order of the heavens. Therefore, while, on the one hand, that religion which is allied to the knowledge and study of nature deserves to be preached and extended, yet the roots of superstition must be steadily weeded out. For superstition is a menace which is always upon you, pressing, driving, pursuing, wherever you turn, when you hear some fortune-teller or some ominous sound, or when you offer a sacrifice, or see a bird fly, or catch sight of a Chaldean or an Etruscan soothsayer, or if it lightens or thunders, if something is struck by lightning, if anything portentous is born or made; some of all these things are continually happening and you are never allowed to rest with a quiet mind'.

Now if we were concerned merely with the beliefs of the most thoughtful minds, I might well stop here and proceed, as my brilliant friend Professor E. K. Rand has done,[2] to leap over four or five centuries and trace the teaching of Cicero in some of the best writings of the Fathers of the Christian Church. But that would be

[1] Cic. *de Diu.* 2. 72. 148–149.
[2] In his wise and delightful book, *The Founders of the Middle Ages*, 1928.

to desert the theme of these essays. It would entirely overlook, what is at least as important, the growth of the religious ideas in the minds of the mass of people during the epoch in which paganism was dying out and Christianity beginning to make its way. To find some picture of the stages by which the grosser superstitions of the pagan world were gradually lifted, or transformed, in the popular mind, we must look not to philosophers but to poets; above all, to one great poet, of whom it may be said that in him we find reflected everything that was noblest in the life of the pagan world, and that from him we can trace the course of everything that survived from that world, to blend with the life of the new. I mean, of course, the poet Vergil. What was Vergil's attitude towards this Greek invasion?

The answer is quite clear. Vergil was eager to promote it and extend it, to press Greek tradition into the service of Roman and Italian life, and his reasons for this attitude are not difficult to see. The Greek myths are generally beautiful and more human than any part of the old Italian folklore. Many of them, too, are enshrined in beautiful works of art, like the statues of Laocoon and Niobe and of the Birth of Venus, which were as familiar to Vergil and thousands of his countrymen as they are to the modern visitor in Rome. And all these stories were linked to some of the greatest parts of Greek poetry. For these reasons the Greek myths gave a totally new interest to religion and even to the operations of life upon which the old Italian religion was meant to bear. That old religion was as dull as a Buddhist prayer-mill; and here came a flood of pretty stories giving life to the objects of worship and adding even a whisper of life after death for the worshipper. So it is not really misleading, although of course the likeness must not be pressed, to describe the *Georgics*, Vergil's picture and praise of a farmer's life, as a missionary poem, intended to raise the farmer's thought about his work to a more human level.

That was all very well. So long as you are only handling stocks and stones and plants and cattle it will not upset your habits of daily piety to call your patron deities by Greek names and to invest them with a halo of Greek romance. But it was quite another thing to contemplate a historical epic whose purpose was to show the divine origin and god-given mission of Rome, beginning far back in the world of Greek legend with the story of Troy, and all the legends of gods and heroes which it implied. In such a poem, which was to end with the actual Rome of Vergil's day, governing the whole world visibly before men's eyes, everything depended on carrying the reader with you. How was this to be done if you took as part of your programme a mass of Greek myth— Kronos, who devoured his own children, and Zeus, who bullied his wife, and threatened to throw her into Hell, and Apollo and Artemis killing Niobe's children because she had boasted that those children were more beautiful than they? How was all this stuff to be connected with a serious national epic?

Well, we must begin by observing what Vergil's own religion was. In this we have no difficulty, because he has given it to us in noble words. It was a kind of pantheism differing from other forms of that vague doctrine by being deeply in earnest and devout. He expresses it in the Fourth Book of the *Georgics* after he has been describing the wonderful intelligence of the bees, and the way in which they plan the life of their hives.[1]

> 'Out of such tokens certain thinkers, tracing
> These powers to their source, declare that bees
> Have share in some divine intelligence,
> Drafts of aetherial spirit; God himself
> Moves, so they tell us, at the heart of all
> Earth and the spreading sea and depth of sky;
> Hence beasts and men, cattle and creatures wild
> Draw each at birth the delicate breath of life
> And to this source return; and so dissolved
> All things rejoin their native element
> And leave no room for death, but living fly
> To make the tale of starry fires complete
> And take once more their places, high in heaven.'

Some of those who read these pages have, I doubt not, many times taken pleasure in the clear reflection of this passage by Wordsworth in his lines on Tintern Abbey:

> A sense sublime
> Of something far more deeply interfused
> Whose dwelling is the light of setting suns,
> And the round ocean, and the living air,
> And the blue sky, and in the mind of man:
> A motion and a spirit that impels
> All thinking things, all objects of all thought,
> And rolls through all things.

Now that is Vergil's point of view, which you may call pantheistic and monotheistic with equal truth. It is

---

[1] Georg. iv. 219–227:

> His quidam signis atque haec exempla secuti,
> Esse apibus partem diuinae mentis et haustus
> Aetherios dixere; deum namque ire per omnes
> Terrasque tractusque maris caelumque profundum;
> Hinc pecudes, armenta, uiros, genus omne ferarum,
> Quemque sibi tenues nascentem arcessere uitas;
> Scilicet huc reddi deinde ac resoluta referri
> Omnia; nec morti esse locum, sed uiua uolare
> Sideris in numerum atque alto succedere caelo.

very close to the philosophy which General Smuts in his eloquent address to the British Association in 1931 called by the name of Holism.

Now with this great conception at heart, how could Vergil deal with all the traditional figures and stories of the Greek myths? Let us begin by putting aside the only two figures among the gods who, in Vergil's story of Aeneas, can be called really divine. I mean those of Jove and Apollo, of whom more later on.

But many other gods remain in the story. How has Vergil dealt with them? The truth is that they are all fully human. Venus and Juno are characters in Vergil's story just as much as Turnus and Mezentius, Evander and Latinus. It would be easy to demonstrate this by quotations from the celestial debate in Book x, in which Juno and Venus employ, brilliantly and with very little scruple, all the devices of human rhetoric to plead their case against and for Aeneas. They are perfectly credible human figures, and the fact that they happen to possess one or two unusual powers, a kind of private telephone to anywhere, a private aeroplane in any element, does not really prevent our understanding them and being interested in their proceedings. But in regard to their doings generally, and those of the other deities, Vergil's method is full of careful thought, of which the different lines have hardly yet been pointed out. The process might be truly described in a striking sentence of Bishop Barnes:

"Religion is kept sweet and wholesome when the flowing waters of reason continually wash away dead fancies, and when the spiritual experience of living men continually revives the truths that come to us from the past".

It was into such a process that Vergil threw himself with

all the power of his genius and all the variety of his imagination. There are some eight different ways in which, in different parts of the Aeneid, Vergil deals with this old-world inheritance; indeed, if we counted the subdivisions of these ways separately, the number[1] would be nearly doubled.

The first is that of open repudiation. To some figures Vergil flatly refuses the name of god altogether.

At the end of Book VIII, in the picture of the Battle of Actium, which Vulcan put upon the shield of Aeneas, there were represented the Egyptian deities who fought for Cleopatra (l. 698):

> Omnigenumque deum monstra et latrator Anubis.
> 'Monsters of gods of all kinds, and the barking Anubis among them.'

A gentler method, but quite as effective, is that of discrediting an old story by referring to its legendary character, and here Vergil uses often the word fama[2] to mean a tale of doubtful truth. Note especially the way in which he deals with the difficult incident of Misenus, the legend of whose death[3] was so closely connected with Cape Misenum, close to the Sybil's cave, that it could not be omitted altogether. Misenus, a follower of Aeneas, and also his trumpeter, was drowned just before Aeneas made his descent into the Underworld. Legend said that the sea god Triton, jealous of the skill Misenus had in blowing the trumpet, swept him off a rock where he was practising at full blast, into the

---

[1] One or two of these, especially the psychological and naturalistic explanations, and the use of dreams, were admirably traced by Professor Richard Heinze in his *Epische Technik*, pp. 308–312; but the others, so far as I know, are here collected for the first time.

[2] Aen. vi. 14; ix. 79.   [3] Aen. vi. 173.

silent sea. Note what Vergil adds to this story, the brief comment *si credere dignum est*, 'if the tale be worth believing'.

A similar expedient is to treat the incident with a touch of humour. This is especially common in the Books with odd numbers, which, as I have shown elsewhere,[1] are of a lighter and gayer texture than the Books with even numbers. Thus in Book v the old story of the prophecy which said that when Aeneas reached the site of his future city he would be reduced by famine to eat his tables (*mensas*) and its fulfilment by their eating the big square sacrificial biscuits which were known by that name, is brought to its climax by an exclamation from the boy Iulus, who regards the matter as an occasion for mirth, and so, Vergil hints, should the reader. Just the same may be said of the episode in which Juno bribes Aeolus to raise a storm by promising him the brightest of her nymphs to marry. Well, if Aeolus came by a new wife every time he made a storm, he must have had a complicated household and a very extensive cave! The story is delightful enough to the schoolboy and to every reader at first sight; but it is impossible surely to suppose that Vergil meant either the wives of Aeolus or the biscuits of Iulus to be taken as a serious part of the history of Rome. For an explicit statement of the atti- tude of thoughtful Romans to such stories, turn to the preface of Livy's history, and remember that Livy, like Vergil, came from Venetian country, and, if not actually his friend, was certainly an eager student of the *Aeneid*.

Another simple way of dealing with unpalatable myths was what I will call 'depresentation', that is, throwing

[1] *Vergil's Creative Art* in British Academy Proceedings, 1931.

them back into a far distant past. All the amours of the gods, which in one of his earlier writings[1] he had described as dating from chaos, when they have to be named in the *Aeneid* as, for example, in the case of poor Juturna,[2] who actually possessed a temple in Rome, all appear as fragments of very ancient history. Like many eminent persons, masculine deities had sown their wild oats a long, long time ago.

We turn to a more interesting method of explanation, which, however, I may dismiss briefly, because it is evident when once pointed out. Supernatural figures are often given a naturalistic or allegorical colour. Thus Iris, the messenger of the gods, is openly identified with the rainbow,[3] and the Centaur from the snow-mountains is, if I am right, clearly described as an avalanche.[4] Or the supernatural figures come in dreams, as when the river Tiber appears to Aeneas in a vision most naturally suggested by his surroundings before he went to sleep.[5]

Rather more subtle, but quite as plain, are the psychological allegories, such as the picture of Fame,[6] with as many eyes and ears and tongues as she has feathers in her wings, who flies shrieking by night, and by day sits on the house-tops or on a tall tower, terrifying great cities. Other obvious examples are Allecto,[7] the personification of hatred, and of Sleep, with his branch dipped in the water of Lethe.[8]

[1] The Epyllion contained in Georg. iv. (345–348).
[2] Aen. xii. 878, a noteworthy passage for many reasons.
[3] Aen. ix. 15–20.   [4] Aen. vii. 674.
[5] Aen. viii. 62.   [6] Aen. iv. 173.
[7] Aen. vii. 345.
[8] Aen. v. 840. The case of Cupid in Book i (710) taking the place of the child Ascanius is another obvious allegory. Dido fondles the little boy and reflects how he embodies the charm of his father Aeneas.

Another form of explanation appears where Vergil suggests a less gross interpretation of some curious incident than that which had been commonly attached to it by popular superstition. Thus, at the memorial ceremonies of Anchises,[1] Aeneas is much encouraged by the appearance of a snake from beneath his father's tomb, which eats the offerings that have been placed upon the tomb, and then departs without injuring any of the onlookers. Now the common belief,[2] certainly of the Greeks, was that the snake at a tomb embodied the spirit of the dead, hence the regular symbolism of two snakes,[3] and this Vergil does not directly repudiate; but he suggests a better alternative. Aeneas, he tells us, was 'uncertain whether to think that the snake was the spirit of the place' (*genius loci*), i.e. his father's own spirit, 'or (merely) some attendant on his father' (*famulus parentis*). This is a typical example of the gentleness with which Vergil handles popular beliefs.

Another very common expedient, of which I have collected over thirty examples from the *Aeneid*,[4] is to give two causes to the same event, one natural, the other supernatural; in the second Book, when Aeneas sees Troy in flames and hears the crash of falling walls, he thinks it is the Greeks who are making havoc of the city; but when Venus opens his eyes, he discovers that it is the gods who are actually at work, Pallas with her thunder cloud, Neptune with his trident,[5] completing

---

[1] Aen. v. 95.

[2] For the origin of the connexion between snakes and life after death and with the healing art generally, see now Sir James Frazer's edition of Ovid's *Fasti* (1929), vol. ii. 295; vol. iv. 321.

[3] Persius, I. 113.

[4] *Vergilian Age*, p. 100 ff.   [5] Aen. ii. 603–616.

the ruin of the doomed city. So when Aeneas is attacked by seven brothers at once, some of their darts are beaten back by his shield and helmet, but others are turned aside by Venus.[1] So we are given the cause of the fall of Troy doubly. The fates of the gods, and the Trojans' own mind, were both bent to their destruction.

Notice finally the limitations which Vergil seems to set to his use of the miraculous. When the gods appear upon the scene to advise or comfort the mortal persons of the story, they always take the form of some particular mortal. Venus appears as a Tyrian huntress,[2] Juno takes the form of Beroe.[3] Otherwise they perform only minor actions, for example, when Juno herself pushes open the Gates of War.[4] We have noted already their frequent appearance in dreams, and the greater freedom in introducing supernatural machinery, which Vergil seems to have allowed himself in the Books with odd numbers, as in the storm raised by Aeolus in Book I, in the miracle of the Bleeding Bush in Book III, and in the conversion of the fleet into sea-nymphs in Book IX. In all these cases the miraculous form may be called ornamental. It is by no means essential to the story.

But when these different methods of reducing his story to something like rational shape had all been applied, more remained, behind or within the theme which Vergil had chosen, namely, the purpose of Providence in founding Rome and developing the Roman Empire. In this there was a stubborn core of orthodox religious belief which could not be denied, or minimised, or

[1] Aen. x. 331.   [2] Aen. i. 315.
[3] Aen. v. 620. Contrast the behaviour of Poseidon in Il. xxi. 288.
[4] Aen. vii. 622.

treated lightly, or explained away. Julius Caesar himself and his heir Augustus continually reminded men of their claim to descend through Aeneas from the goddess Venus, and what seemed to the Romans the visible activity of Jove in the triumphant history of their empire was represented by his temple on the Capitol, the most sacred spot in Rome. These things, therefore, Vergil must accept; but he accepts them, with significant silence, as part of the greater mystery of things. We learn, of course, of the prayers which Aeneas offers to his divine mother; but we learn also how constantly she refuses to meet him on ordinary human terms: as soon as he recognises her she vanishes at once. She is his mother, no doubt; but we have no recollections of a childhood in which she played towards her child the mother's part, nor a wife's part to her husband Anchises. The myth is preserved; but it is carefully kept far from the atmosphere of common daylight.

Observe, too, how the hill which was destined to become the Capitol is first mentioned—'this hill with tree-covered summit', 'a place of dread sanctity'; the countrymen trembled before the cliff and its crown of forest. 'It is the dwelling of a god, though what god they know not.'[1]

This or that detail in these different methods may have seemed surprising or unconvincing. But I venture to hope that on reviewing the survey the reader will realise that it does provide evidence beyond dispute of the set purpose with which Vergil employed these different ways of dealing with the burden of old-world superstition; he cannot have devised so many different means without

[1] Aen. viii. 352.

deliberate intention. If any doubt remains in our minds, we need only contrast with Vergil's studied workmanship the totally different way in which such a poet as Ovid handles the same kind of legend. In Ovid we have everywhere the frankly sceptical tone of the jesting teller of good stories, revelling in the primitive absurdity of tales of the gods which no one, so he reckons, will take seriously in any sense whatever.

Little room is left me to speak of the two really divine figures in Vergil's story, Jove and Apollo. Jove, as we have seen, could not be acquitted of certain failings in the past; but all he says and does in the *Aeneid* itself is dignified and noble. He is the ideal Roman father who lives to serve his country, that is, mankind, by maintaining the moral law, and like a Roman father, he must himself bow to its inscrutable decrees. He is very little removed from the Stoic conception, which we may call with equal correctness Providence or Fate. He is the great constraining and restraining power that limits men's action by certain bounds; he is the negative aspect of " the power without us, not ourselves ".

But that is not the whole of Vergil's picture of real deity. The positive, inspiring, stimulating spirit, which moves men to noble thoughts and noble deeds, was in Apollo, the god of perpetual youth. It is Apollo who inspires Iulus in his first battle. He imparts the gifts of music and song and the power of healing. Above all, he is the god of revelation, he declares the divine will to men. At Delos and later, it is he that commands Aeneas to seek Italy, and it was under the guidance of his Sibyl that Aeneas descended to see his father in the Underworld and received the full prophecy of the greatness of

Rome. As we know, to the Greek mind Apollo represented everything that was humane and enlightened in
their conception of divinity; and it is to be counted for
righteousness as well as for prudent policy to Octavian
that he chose this Greek god, comparatively new to Rome,
as his patron all through his career, attributing to him,
no doubt sincerely enough, the greatest of his victories,
and establishing in his honour the greatest monument of
imperial power and wisdom that Rome was destined to
see, the magnificent temple and library on the Palatine
Hill.

What, then, was the revelation which, in the supreme
Book of his epic, Vergil represents as given to his hero
by Apollo's command? For our present purpose two
passages, both quite short, stand out from the rest of
Book VI, and it is noteworthy that neither of them is put
into the mouth of the Sibyl. Just as Dante later on in
the third and highest chapter of his vision received his
instruction from Beatrice, no longer from the guide who
had conducted him through Hell and Purgatory, so
Aeneas, when he reaches Elysium, is taught, partly by
his father Anchises, and partly from what he sees by his
own eyes. Anchises gives him the new ideal of public
life, strongly marked by Roman limits and yet touched
with more than merely Roman thought, the famous declaration of what Rome is to do for the world, ending
with the great command to establish peace and subdue
those who abhorred it.

> 'Others, I well believe, with finer touch
> Shall kindle breath in forms of bronze, and mould
> Faces of marble all aglow with life.
> Others may plead with greater eloquence,
> Make chart of heaven and time the rising stars.

> But choose thou, son of Rome, the imperial task
> To rule the peoples; this shall be thy art,
> Show mercy to the humble, crush the proud,
> Make peace and teach the nations how to live.'

Beside this, perhaps one may say beyond it, Vergil gives us his ideal of private conduct in the list of those who attain the highest reward in Heaven, the snow-white chaplet. This is the most intimate part of the whole revelation, and Vergil felt, somehow, constrained to give it to us in his own words, and not through any one of his characters.

> 'Here moved a host of spirits who had passed
> Suffering wounds to save their fatherland,
> Priests who had kept unsullied purity
> Lifelong, and faithful prophets whose response
> Had never shamed Apollo's oracle;
> Those found new arts, and left the world more fair;
> These by good service left a memory
> Cherished by two or three; but all the host
> Bore on their temples chaplets bright as snow.'

A curious thing has happened to these lines in our own time, as if to make it clearer than ever what Vergil meant. In the translation which Professor Eduard Norden of Berlin added to his great edition of Book VI, he made a striking insertion, so that the last and highest class of the blessed was restricted to "die Herrscher", 'the lords of men'. Norden was thinking of emperors and kings whose subjects cherished their memory with gratitude. (In his second edition he changed the word *Herrscher* into *Edlen*, 'nobles', which makes little difference.) There is no such limitation in Vergil's line, which literally rendered is 'those who made two or three people remember them by good service', *merendo*, 'by serving'—the simplest of all words. The snow-white chaplet is an honour which indeed an emperor might covet; but in Vergil's heaven it is one which a slave could win. That is the highest point of the revelation granted to men by the most divine of all the figures that Vergil's genius could conceive, the most perfect impersonation of the mission of Rome.

CHAPTER V

MODERN PROBLEMS IN THE EYES OF
AN AUGUSTAN POET

I N the preceding chapters the subjects on which I have touched may be called roughly theological. That is to say, they have been concerned mainly with the beliefs which were held in different parts of Ancient Italy at different times, about the nature of deity and of the relations between men and those unseen powers; especially of the beliefs that men entertained of what the gods might do for them or to them in this life and the next. To-day I want to descend, though some might call it ascending, from the region of more or less speculative thought to what are called practical questions of conduct. Yet, in fact, in forming our judgments of what is right and wrong in human life, here and now, the life of the individual in his home and family, and his life in the wider unities or organisms to which he belongs; in considering these ethical problems, though we touch more nearly questions which demand an answer from us in action, we have by no means deserted the region of thought. For I suppose there is no department of philosophic or religious theory in which more depends upon the point of view from which we start; no part of life, in fact, in which what our Oxford friends call Values have a more direct effect, whether we are fully conscious of it or not, upon our own conduct in some of the gravest matters that we ever have to handle. Nor can it,

when we reflect upon the nature of the teaching with
which Christianity has been associated, be irrelevant
to its history to dwell for a little on some of the Values
which stood highest in the noblest minds of the age
which immediately preceded the beginning of Christian
teaching. Certainly it cannot seem irrelevant to consider
in this light some of the ethical problems which have
been earnestly and often fiercely, not to say cruelly, discussed in many centuries, and to which few men in our
own time would dare to say that a final answer had been
formulated, when we remember that, in one form or
another, they were forced upon the notice and deeply
considered in the teaching of Christ himself; and that one
set of them in particular, the problems connected with
national sentiment, were the immediate cause of the
tragedy by which His life on earth was brought to an end.

Yet it may well be, I am afraid, that some of those
who have seen this title have contemplated, not without
a certain sense of amusement, a professor of an ancient
language undertaking to discourse on any ethical problem of the modern world; for some of those who read
this essay may be conscious of a feeling—which I know
exists though its owners are rarely bold enough to express it—that there can be nothing in any writer of
antiquity which is worth the study of men and women
in this enlightened age or likely to contain any wisdom
or stimulus that cannot be found more fully in writers
nearer our own time, whom, so they think, they can
understand without the trouble of knowing the earlier
sources of what those writers had to say. To such critics
I will only say with Themistocles, 'Strike me, but hear
me'. And perhaps in the end they will not be ill-pleased

to discover that some of the world's wisdom is older
than they thought, and that it was first conceived under
different skies and in a different social order, and yet
possesses a light and a power which to neglect is to im-
poverish the life of mankind.

But some, perhaps, who could not make any criticism
that springs merely from ignorance, may still wonder
whether the difference, of age and conditions of life,
between our own epoch and that in which the poet Vergil
lived is not so vast and disconcerting as to make it un-
fruitful to apply any judgments of his to problems which
face us now. And if any one suggested that an ancient
poet had conceived a sentiment, or had framed any kind
of principle bearing on any of our own questions, these
critics might shrug their shoulders and think that the
lecturer was reading some doctrine of his own into the
utterance of a poet who was remote from the ideas to
which the doctrine was now applied.

That criticism contains a caution which students of
literature in any age must take to heart. They can only
avoid the danger which it deprecates, they can only be
honest to their author and to their hearers, if they study
what their author said closely in relation to the conditions in which he said it. It has been the misfortune
of every great book, not excepting some of the most
sacred, that particular portions and texts have been torn
from their context, divorced altogether from the life in
which their author first conceived them and to which
he was conscious that they referred, and then applied,
sometimes with amazing results, to circumstances entirely different. We must not open the pages of Vergil
or of Plato with the superstition of a Stuart king, to find

some cryptic utterance of Fate which will tell us whether to go into exile or to stay and fight our adversaries. We must humbly be content to master as completely as we can the events and beliefs of the world in which the poet wrote before we can be confident that we have seized the deepest feeling which inspired his work.

But when we have done this, when we know the political facts and the social feelings of the epoch in which Vergil wrote, if we discover an essential likeness between the crisis on which he brought to bear his own reflection; his own quickening reproof; his own stimulating faith in the essential goodness of human nature, if only its best impulses could be, not stifled, but directed and used—an essential likeness, I say, between that crisis and the problems of our own world, a likeness based not on any superficial resemblance of particular events, but on the fundamental laws and instincts of our mortal lot; then, I hope, it will not be wasted time to ask what response the problems of that crisis drew from the thought of a supreme poet—supreme above all in the tender and intimate depth of his knowledge of the human soul.

Perhaps I have dwelt too long in meeting doubts which the reader may be willing to lay aside, at least for a brief space; and I must go on to explain what the problems are which were in any sense shared by Vergil's day with ours. Every one knows that society in his day as in ours had undergone a terrible experience, had been shaken, as the phrase goes, to its foundations. What is right? What is wrong? Is there such a thing as right and wrong? Can human government or even private human conduct ever hope to decide? And when it has decided, can it hope to follow out its decision?

In two aspects of life especially, it seems to me, this atmosphere of doubt besets us, and they are aspects which involved problems for thinking men in Vergil's time too; how to regard and to direct first, the relations between different nations; and secondly, the relations between the two sexes.

Let no one think that I am representing a great poet as having laid down instructions or developed doctrines, which can be explicitly put into words, as having said to his contemporaries " Do this—do that" ; "Approve this measure"—"condemn that" ; "Execrate such and such a person" ; "Applaud all the work of such another". A great imaginative writer does not work like that. What he does is to conceive a story and work it out in a series of clear and poignant pictures which live in men's memory and by their silent beauty continually compel men to ask, "Why did this happen? What was the ultimate cause of this happiness, or this tragedy?"—which convince them, in a way that no mere words can do, that so long as men persist in such and such beliefs, such and such conventions, such and such ambitions, so long the end will be what the poet has portrayed. And if we find that these beliefs, these conventions, these ambitions, and their results in what men do and suffer are no less common, no less powerful in our own day than in Vergil's; if we find indeed that these springs and motives of action are so far spread, so nearly universal in society to-day that we assume them almost as a matter of course; that we cannot believe—as certainly the men of Vergil's day could not believe, nor do the greatest part of his interpreters to-day understand—that Vergil doubted our habits of thought and questioned the validity of our conventions—then perhaps we shall find it worth our while to realise with him, if we can, what the fruit of these things has been and will always be.

Indeed, to those of us who are concerned—and which of us is not?—with the conditions of the world to-day, when we see it still at the mercy of the customs and motives whose outcome Vergil has portrayed, it must seem one of the highest ends of education for our younger generation to master the experience of the ancient world; to know something for themselves of the wisdom of the Greek thinkers who had before them the spectacle of a whole group of political experiments, each of them tried out to the end; and not less to know something of the history in which that Greek thought found its finest development, namely, the growth of Rome; to know something of the collapse of that government as a re-public under stress of the passions which Vergil depicts; and to recognise the power of the ideas which rescued it from chaos and made its Empire the cradle of all the civilisation which humanity has yet achieved. It is hard indeed not to feel a certain impatience—to use no stronger word—with those who, in face of the similar calamities which have befallen and still threaten the life of the world to-day—in face of the financial and social distress in which all its governments find themselves at this moment—can calmly tell us that an adequate basis for education is to be sought in the quiet walks of natural science or the unquiet ocean of economics, or even in the abstractions of a political philosophy which omits from its study the whole of ancient history and the greatest part of human letters. The chaos of A.D. 1933 only too closely resembles the chaos of 33 B.C., and if we are to be saved from more terrible struggles than were needed to bring order back into the world in that generation, we cannot afford to neglect the spiritual teaching which delivered it then.

The story of Dido is the romance of the *Aeneid*, and in one of the poems to which Vergil looked back as giving him a kind of model—the *Odyssey* of Homer—there were romances too. The main theme of the *Odyssey* is the return of the hero to his faithful wife; and the poet, who was clearly familiar with the experiences of sailors, chose by one of the most charming touches of genius in epic poetry to represent the loves of Odysseus as immortal goddesses who, however beautiful, however irresistible, in their own ways and in their own little islands, could never rival in his heart the fair image of his wife at home. Starting from this happy expedient, Homer so shapes his story that both these divine ladies, Circe and Calypso, should themselves speed their lover on his way, and that the decree of separation should be sent by the highest authority not to the hero, but to each hostess herself in turn. Such is the simple melodrama of the story in Homer.

What has Vergil made of it? We shall find that the art of the epic has discovered and conquered a new world of thought and passion since it was content with the placid farewells of Calypso and Circe.

Vergil's originality nowhere appears more clearly than in the great romance of the *Aeneid*, the story of Queen Dido. By all tradition Carthage was founded nearly four hundred years later than the fall of Troy. Yet it is only seven or eight years after that fall that Vergil's hero is cast on the African coast.[1] Those who know the story best will, I think, be least unwilling to hear it again.

In the midst of his wanderings from Troy, which he left in flames to follow an obscure divine command to found a new city in the West, Aeneas suffers shipwreck through a storm raised by his enemy, the goddess Juno. The storm sinks one of his ships and divides the rest so that they are driven ashore at two different points of the African coast, neither of which is far from the new city of Carthage, which was being built by a band of colonists from Tyre, themselves exiles led by Queen Dido. She had fled from Tyre because her husband had been murdered by her own brother, who had then usurped the throne. Aeneas, after adventures which rouse his hopes and courage again after the grievous loss which his small band of exiles has suffered, discovers the new city and thus sees Dido's work before he sees her; and amidst the crowd, actually watches her discharge the duties of a queen, presiding, directing, judging. And the story is so contrived that Dido hears of Aeneas from a band of his followers from the part of the fleet separated from Aeneas himself, who naturally suppose that Aeneas is lost. Dido welcomes them in a queenly speech, promising to protect them and inquiring for the fate of their famous leader.

At this cardinal moment the hero himself appears, glorified by his mother's divine magic with a glow of youth. Of course, we see the result. An exchange of warm-hearted courtesy, the attachment of the Queen to little Iulus, Aeneas's son, the boyish image of his father,

---

[1] It is possible that the poet Naevius may have invented the idea of Aeneas' landing at Carthage; but it is certain that he did not invent the romance of Dido.

lead up to a royal banquet in honour of the strangers. Here Aeneas tells the long story of the fall of Troy, of the death of his wife Creusa, and of his travels since. Throughout he leaves his own prowess modestly unmentioned, though he dwells on the great command which he lives to carry out: to found a greater Troy in the West.

The fourth Book of the *Aeneid* begins on the morning after this great narration has reached its close. Dido confesses to her sister Anna how deeply she has been moved by the nobleness of her guest; yet she protests that she is resolved to be faithful to the memory of her murdered husband Sychaeus. But her sister, the prototype of every confidante in European drama, bids her relinquish such scruples and marry Aeneas. 'Do you think', she asks in irony, 'that the buried dead will care, or even if they do, do you think that the jealous powers around you— your brother Pygmalion in Tyre and Iarbas of the Numidian desert—will suffer you to remain unmarried? No. For your very people's sake, ally yourself to the Trojan.'

From this point the story moves rapidly, picturing Dido's growing passion and her changing moods of restless longing and self-reproach. She has no heart for her wonted pursuits. All the building of the city is interrupted. The walls are empty of workers, and the gaunt levers and cranes stand out motionless against the sky. The crisis comes through a plot of the two rival deities, Juno and Venus. The rivals agree from precisely opposite motives. Juno hopes to prevent the founding of Rome by keeping Aeneas at Carthage; she cares nothing for Aeneas. Venus hopes to protect Aeneas; she cares nothing for Dido. Both their designs, as Vergil makes clear, are disappointed; but for the moment they have their way. The treachery of the goddesses prevails over one mortal woman.

A great hunt in the hills, which Dido has planned, is broken by a thunderstorm and the two lovers come from different paths to shelter in a cave. Their followers scatter far away. 'Forthwith Juno, Goddess of Wedlock, gave the word for their union, and the nymphs cried aloud from the hilltops. Wedlock, Dido calls it, so she veils her weakness.'[1]

And straightway rumour, swiftest of evils, flies through her kingdom; not her subjects only, but the jealous neighbouring powers learn the truth.

It is a grim picture, this, of the lovers in the twilight of the cave with the storm outside, a wonderfully true imagination of conditions such as alone could overthrow the barriers of convention and self-control. The suggestion of the incident Vergil owed to an earlier poet, Apollonius Rhodius, in whose epic of Jason and Medea a cave is made to serve as a sort of Gretna Green, a convenient spot for a private but legitimate and not wholly secret marriage. Apollonius, who was a rather dainty writer with a sense of the proprieties, lays stress on the decorum of the proceedings by representing Jason's soldiers as standing sentinels outside, and the cave as having been previously inhabited; and he tells us that the friendly Queen Arete, who planned the marriage, sent a supply of furniture into the cave, especially of

---

[1] The weakness that Vergil recognises and which he calls *culpa*—not by any harsher name—was not her alliance with Aeneas in itself, but her having abandoned her faithfulness to the memory of her former husband. She was no longer *uni nupta uiro*, which was the distinction of every Roman widow in the great times.

soft linen. Vergil's picture has no such ludicrous ac-
cessories. The remoteness, the silence, the darkness of
the cave and the roar of the storm outside are all
essential to Vergil's story; *summoque ulularunt uertice
nymphae*—'the nymphs shrieked and shouted from the
hilltops.' The lovers are in the grasp of cosmic powers
greater than themselves; in no other way, we feel, could
the drama have been accomplished.

The picture has sunk deep into men's imagination.
Shakespeare dwells on it in *The Tempest*; and readers of
modern fiction may remember how it suggested to Émile
Zola the most intense scene in his grim romance of the
mines.

But though the forebodings are dark, for the moment
rosy light is round the lovers. Dido cares little for her
buildings now; though Aeneas has begun to be interested
in them as a royal consort.

Then comes the summons from Jove himself. Stirred,
as Vergil rather allows[1] than gives us to believe, by the
prayers of his African son, the Moor Iarbas, who is a
suitor for Dido's hand, Jove sends Mercury with orders to
Aeneas: 'He is to sail; that is all. Tell him that from me'.

When Mercury arrives, he finds Aeneas arrayed in the
uniform of a Tyrian general building houses and planning
forts; and Mercury's first word of reproach is that he is
behaving like a husband—*uxorius*—building a 'pretty
city' for his wife and forgetting his own promised land.
This reproof Aeneas painfully admits. His duty to his
son and his people is the challenge to his conscience
which forces him to face the pain of leaving Dido.

Observe the psychological meaning which so often,

[1] *dicitur*, l. 204.

as we have[1] seen, underlies Vergil's use of supernatural machinery. The appearance of Mercury represents the duty which Aeneas has forgotten. He is watching walls being built and the thought comes to him that they are not being built for his son nor for the Trojans, but for some successor of Dido; and this, no doubt, was felt by the Trojans who were helping in the work, like the Israelites building pyramids for Pharaoh. Aeneas is horror-struck and prepares sadly to obey. Knowing Dido's passionate nature, he dreads to tell her and deems it wise to prepare his fleet for sailing before he confesses his intention. But, of course, she finds it out otherwise and turns upon Aeneas, reproaching him with his treachery, and beseeching him to stay. When he refuses, she wildly professes disbelief in his divine commission and prophesies vengeance upon him. At the height of this second outburst, she falls fainting in her servant's arms.

Aeneas, 'though shaken by the great tide of his love', and longing to comfort her, still pursues as in a dream the divine bidding, which his followers, for their part, gladly execute. Dido sends entreaties to him by her sister, but in vain; his purpose stands like an oak rooted in a hollow of some Alpine cliff.

Overwhelmed by her calamity, Dido prays for death. She bids her bridal bed and all the gifts of Aeneas to be set on a funeral pyre in the inner court of her palace; it is a magical charm, she says, to bring about the death of her betrayer. One more night she spends in sleepless questioning whether she dare desert her kingdom and accompany Aeneas alone or whether she shall summon her subjects and bid them desert their half-built city and

[1] See p. 89.

follow her to Italy. She concludes that her only escape must be in death. 'A fitting punishment', she cries, 'for my broken faith to Sychaeus!'

Next day, when she sees the fleet actually sailing, she invokes a terrible curse on Aeneas and on the race he is to found, and then stabs herself upon the pyre, praying with her last utterance that Aeneas may see the flames.

Such is the story. Its subject is the conflict between the claims of love and the claims of public duty. Hear the effect which it has produced upon a distinguished scholar, who cries out with the vehemence of one who feels pain but does not understand its source, a criticism of value just because of its sincerity:

> Once only [says Dr T. E. Page] Aeneas exhibits human frailty and then it is to show that as a human being he is contemptible. He accepts the love of Dido and then abandons her to despair and death. There is no need to emphasise his crime; Vergil himself has done that. The splendid passage which describes his final interview with the Queen is a master-piece. Dido bursts into an invective which for scorn and tragic grandeur is almost unequalled. Aeneas is left stammering and preparing to say many things, a hero who had, one would think, lost his character for ever....But Vergil seems unmoved by his own genius. How the man who wrote the lines placed in Dido's mouth could immediately after-wards speak of *pius Aeneas*, 'the good Aeneas' is inexplicable.

Well, that is a vigorous challenge. Let us try to take it up. We may notice, by the way, what Dr Page has not observed that this is the first time the epithet *pius*, best translated 'faithful', is applied to Aeneas in this Book. Before this he has been called 'the Trojan leader' and 'the Dardanian child of Venus'; that is, his oriental connexions are made prominent, not his duty to the future Rome. It is clear that Vergil knew what he was doing.

Dr Page's comment expresses the first feeling which the book leaves on the mind of the modern reader; nor is the impression of pain peculiar to us. St Augustine repeats more than once the confession that he wept over the sorrows of Dido when he ought to have been weeping over his own sins. One may doubt whether the second kind of weeping would have done him as much good. In any case, it is clear that that powerful and most human bishop felt his reading of Dido's story was one of the great experiences of life.

What is the essence of the tragedy? Just this: that Aeneas, having yielded to his love for Dido and decided to abandon his political duty for her, is driven by conscience to change his mind and sacrifice her. The answer which such a question has received in different ages varies both with the conception of the ordinary relations of public and private duty and with the conception of the general position of women in human life. On the first of these two points we have to recall what critics of Vergil seem to have forgotten: how much less in the ethics of the ancient world than in modern sentiment, the happiness of the individual counted as against the national welfare. It was a matter of course to any ancient moralist that private happiness could not be weighed against the claims of an empire or even of a city. Vergil puts this doctrine on the lips of Aeneas, who humbly accepts it. But what is Vergil's comment? We shall see.

On the second point—the position of women—observe only that what we call chivalry, the spirit which we learned to love in the Black Knight of *Ivanhoe* or in *Quentin Durward*, in which men take it as their duty to protect women, not because they are to reap any reward themselves, but just because women are human creatures whose physical weakness needs defence, is a conception which, as the name reminds us, had still to wait some eleven centuries to win any general acceptance. It was rare in the ancient world, where, in the time of Caesar no less than that of Pericles, whenever a town was captured, women were spared from slaughter only to be sold as slaves.

Consider briefly the answers given to these questions by the politicians, by the general society of Vergil's time, and by Vergil himself. The first would have been brief and reassuring. Suppose we had the privilege of cross-examining Mark Antony or Augustus about what they thought of such a case as Dido's. Antony would have replied with the brutality that appears in a letter of his recorded by Suetonius, and Augustus with a bland air of philosophic detachment; but their answers would have been the same. Nobody was to blame except, perhaps, Dido herself; another moth had singed her wings, that was all. Women were things with which the politicians must reckon; indeed, they were often very useful, but when the use for them was over, the less said the better.

More than one example had been seen of this in the last thirty years of the Republic. The most conspicuous was the case of Cleopatra, whose beauty first ruined Julius Caesar—for it was her living in Rome[1] in Caesar's gardens across the Tiber, which Mommsen and other modern historians have strangely omitted to notice, that

[1] Cic. ad Att. 14. 8. 1 and 20. 2; 15. 15. 2; Dio Cassius, 43. 27 (46 B.C.).

more than anything else created the fierce unpopularity which permitted Julius Caesar to be murdered. Later on Cleopatra had quite ruined Mark Antony. Augustus had learned wisdom from this. He refused to see Cleopatra, though he had taken her prisoner; and this, as Shakespeare knew, was the cause of her suicide. This story is quite clearly reflected in the picture of Dido's death when Aeneas has departed, having steadfastly refused to see her again.

But Augustus had learned more positive lessons. Probably there was never a ruler who made more heartless use of women to further his political schemes. He was himself betrothed four times and married three, and in all cases the repudiation was made by him. Nor was he any more scrupulous in his treatment of his sister, his daughter and his heirs. In 40 B.C. he pawned the hand of his sister Octavia to the drunken ruffian Mark Antony. In 27 B.C. when his great commander Agrippa, to whom he owed his victories, was 36 years old, he was forced to put away his wife Pomponia in order to marry the Emperor's niece Marcella, a child of fifteen; and, seven years later, she was divorced in her turn in order that he might marry the Emperor's daughter Julia, who was then 19 years old. She, however, was already a widow, having been married when she was 14 years old to the Emperor's nephew. All this happened under Vergil's eyes in the years in which he was writing the *Aeneid*.

But you will say that the politician is apt to reduce moral questions to their lowest terms. What was the view of decent Roman society? The generation which saw and sympathised with Cicero's passionate grief at the death of his daughter; which saw the devoted affec-

tion with which Turia saved her husband through the
long terror of the proscription[1] of the year 43, was not
altogether careless of human affection. But the tie between the sexes, either in marriage or outside it, did
not normally involve any bond of affection strong enough
to imply a life-long companionship. Not merely emperors, but upright and benevolent men, regarded divorce
for any one of many causes as a natural thing. The husband of Turia, in the delightful story of her life which
he engraved upon marble, counts it as an example of her
goodness that she proposed to him to divorce her because
she was childless. The ordinary educated Roman of
Vergil's day would have judged it monstrous to suppose
that a woman's claim on a man's affection could be
weighed against his political duty, and he would point
to the disasters which befell great men who had defied
Roman opinion on this point.

Clearly, then, no one in Rome—unless it were Vergil
—was prepared to think the worse of Aeneas for what he
had done. What has been continually overlooked is this:
that Vergil's attitude is not represented merely by what
Aeneas says in his defence, but by what he tacitly admits;
and that the actual words put into his mouth, though
they are true and represent the standards of Vergil's
time, contain only part of Vergil's own comment. For,
suppose we grant all that Dr Page can urge. It would
remain true that it is not we who should be condemning
what happened—we, with nineteen Christian centuries,
with a northern habit of mind, with the age of Chivalry,
with the Puritan struggle, all behind us to shape our

[1] See the first of my *Harvard Lectures on the Vergilian Age* (Cambridge,
Mass., 1928) and Warde Fowler's *Social Life in Rome*, p. 159.

judgment; not we, but Vergil himself. If we conclude
that Vergil has represented his hero as a criminal, at
least let us observe that if Vergil did so, it was because
he was twenty centuries in advance of the ethics of his
day.

But how far does he condemn Aeneas himself? Where
does the story go wrong? It begins truly enough. Aeneas
and Dido meet under conditions which show each to the
other in the noblest light. Their love was human and
natural and sprang from the finest parts of both characters.
But the same evil machinery which threw Aeneas on to
Dido's coast is set to work again. Dido is betrayed not
merely by Venus, but by her own sister, who appeals to
political considerations; and the meeting in the cave
arose directly from Juno's devising of the second storm.
Juno, in her eagerness to imprison Aeneas, is false not
merely to her favourite, Dido, but to her own special
duty as the patroness of wedlock. Vergil emphasises this
at the crisis by calling her 'Goddess of Wedlock'. She
wished the union to be permanent, and behaved as if it
could be, though she knew it could not. To Roman sentiment a real marriage with a foreign woman was impossible. What do these goddesses really represent in
Vergil's mind?

Why must Dido die when Aeneas forsakes her? Why
can she not accept the bitterness of their separation as
he does, taking it for an ordinance of inscrutable Providence and continuing her work? Because the conventions of man forbid her. Juno, Venus, Iarbas, Pygmalion
—what do they stand for? Vergil's deepest meaning has
hardly yet been pointed out, and for one simple reason.
Vergil's readers were and are too much under the do-

minion of certain social and national conceptions to dream that Vergil could criticise them; and yet, these conceptions are precisely what Vergil's story has pierced and analysed, stripped of their fine names, and left to be judged by their real human value.

Iarbas, the swarthy neighbour king, is prepared to make an attack upon Dido's new city if she will not marry him; and her brother Pygmalion, though less barbarous, is at one with him in the belief that a woman reigning alone cannot be tolerated. If the man whom Dido loves cannot stay to defend her, she feels that her only escape from barbarism is in death. These are social attitudes which perhaps one may say the world has now at least partly outgrown. But Iarbas and Pygmalion are not the chief factors. Who made the conditions that threw Aeneas and Dido together? Who ordained their separation? Why could not Aeneas take Dido with him, as he half suggested and as she long contemplated? The answer is the same as that which dictated those other bitter alliances and bitter divorces which Vergil saw in the world of his day—*raisons d'état*. It was the conflict of political designs. Juno and Venus embody the ideas of a jealous, narrow nationalism, an essentially anti-human national sentiment—the kind of patriotism to which the prosperity of a neighbouring nation is a positive offense; which holds that two great peoples cannot exist and flourish side by side; a sentiment which old Cato had expressed in his daily imprecation, 'Carthage must be blotted out', a century before Vergil wrote. And perhaps the most important aspect of the century of civil wars, in which the Republic of Rome found a terrible end, was the struggle which they embodied between the old nationalist view, on the one hand, in which the Provinces were simply fields to be exploited by Roman governors, a view still implied in the conduct of Julius Caesar, and on the other hand the newer sense of responsibility to the subject Empire, the new conception of a world community transcending the City State; the conception for which Cicero laboured and pleaded and died.

How near this lies to our whole subject appears at once when we remember that the fiercest enemies of Christ's teaching, the people who were largely responsible for his death, were those ardent Jewish nationalists, the Pharisees, whose bitter zeal would recognise no single fact of their time or of the position of their country which stood in the way of their fanatical faith.

And there are other questions which will suggest themselves to every reader. Was this nationalist passion extinct in Europe in 1914? Is it extinct in the world of 1933?

Were we not recently told on high authority that the policy of a great country in a matter vitally affecting other nations, namely its tariffs, must be determined solely by its own interests? On the direct effect of Protectionist tariffs on national life it is not my business to speak; but it is my duty to plead as plainly and earnestly as I may that this merely nationalist spirit which (wisely or unwisely) they embody, this resolve to use the power of a nation to increase, so it is supposed, the wealth of some members of the nation to the detriment of other nations, is the oldest superstition in all political history; and when enforced by a knot of ignorant and war-loving Prussians in 1914 could not be stopped at any

less cost than the loss of nine million lives, the flower
of a whole generation. What has Vergil to say of this
superstition? What is his comment? His comment is in
the outcome of his story, the climax of the whole Book
—Dido's curse upon Aeneas and on Rome, and its prophecy of Hannibal's invasion of Italy.

> 'Hear me, ye gods, and one day from my dust
> Breed an avenger! Rise thou dread unknown,
> Drive from their promised land with sword and fire
> The Trojan settlers, now or whensoe'er
> The morrow gives thee power, drive and destroy!
> Arms against arms array, tide against wave;
> Embattle continent with continent;
> On them and on their children's children, war!'

Nothing could better show the amazing power of pre-
conceived ideas than the comment made on this passage
by even so thoughtful a scholar as the late Professor
Heinze. 'Dido's curse is, of course, all turned to good.'
Turned to good! What does the curse mean? What
does Vergil represent as the fruit of the plotting of Juno
and Venus? Nothing less than the three deadly wars
between Rome and Carthage—one the longest, one the
most dangerous, and one the most cruel that Rome ever
waged; nothing less than the extinction of Saguntum and
Capua and Carthage, the carnage of Trebia and Trasimene
and Cannae—the terror that walked in Italy for eleven
years and made the name of Hannibal the dread of every
Roman home.

That is the outcome, says Vergil, when men of state
make human affections an instrument of their designs.
Dido's agony sprang not merely from the callousness of
Juno and Venus, but from their motive, the mainspring
of their action: the nationalist, political passion whose

falsehood we find it so hard to outgrow. Have we not ourselves heard the like of her curse from scores of lips when the frenzy of war was upon us?

Listen to Dido's side of the story as Vergil conceived it, and see how clear its challenge is both to the frivolity of self-indulgence and to the cruelty of hard and fast conventions. Its central thought is the sanctity of human affection, a sanctity violated as much by the hardness of social sanctions or of political ambition as by the brutality and selfishness of animal passion. 'Think,' Vergil cries to us; 'realise the infinite consequence that hangs upon your acts; the infinite blessing which the love of men and women was created to achieve for themselves and for their children, and the infinite misery which your blind self-indulgence or your blind enforcement of political designs or conventional rules may make instead.'

> 'What? Did'st thou think to hide this shameful deed,
> Traitor, and steal away without a word?
> Canst thou forget our love? forget the troth
> Thou gav'st me freely once? Canst thou not dream
> What cruel doom awaits me, thou being gone?
> Why—'tis mid-winter; yet thou must away,
> Must bid thy vessels hug the Northern blast?
> Oh, cruel, cruel! Would'st thou e'en if Troy
> Stood as of old and thou wert Troyward bound,
> Would'st thou have launched thy fleet on yon wild surge
> Even for Troy? Ah! 'Tis from me thou flee'st
> If flee thou wilt—O hear me, hear me plead,
> Plead by these tears, by thine own pledged right hand,
> By that poor last appeal that my own act
> Has left me right to utter even yet,
> Our lovers' joy, our bridal song begun:
> If e'er I served thee well, if aught in me
> Had sweetness for thee once, have pity now.
> Pity this royal house, so near its fall,

And, if yet prayer can move thee, I entreat
Put that fell purpose from thee. For thy sake
The Afric peoples bear me enmity
And kings of barbarous tribes; and far away
The lords of Tyre watch for my overthrow.
For thy sake, no man's else, I cast away
My honour, my one pearl of fair renown;
In whose hands dost thou leave me here to die?
Be but my guest again, my friend at least,
Friend, whom I called my husband, yesterday.
What wait I for? Till Tyrian battering-rams
Thunder my brother's wrath on these new walls?
Or Moor Iarbas make me wife and slave?
Ah, but if only first, ere thou had'st fled,
One ray of that dear hope had dawned on me
That beams in mother's eyes; if in these halls
A baby child of ours had danced and smiled,
Smiling his far-off father back again,
Oh, then methinks I were not, as I am,
Utterly, utterly betrayed and lost.'

Here, as everywhere, Vergil brings us face to face with
the mystery of life. Carthage had struggled to the death
with Rome. Aeneas struggles with the world of con-
flicting passions and contradictory fates; and though to
him might be granted some faith or vision of the end to
which the struggle will contribute, yet Dido's great work
is cancelled and his own life is marred. His regret for
Dido remains in the latest glimpse which Vergil gives
us of his heart—'Against my will, O Queen, I left thy
shores'. So he cries to her when he sees her in the
underworld in Book VI. In that after-life Dido is restored to her first love and has left behind her passion for
Aeneas like a bad dream. So in the far-off kingdom of
peace we may believe that there shall be no more
slaughter, nor wars, nor starvation, nor oppression; but

on the human stage the mystery is unsolved—that mystery of human affection which shines through every page that Vergil wrote; the mystery of its double nature, its two sides. The supreme paradox of life to Vergil lay in the fact that no affection can be real which does not make us capable in equal degree of the most exquisite happiness and the most exquisite pain. That is the Golden Bough growing in the darkness of the forest. And while philosophers of many schools may bid us turn away from it in carelessness or fear, Vergil bids us seek it and grasp it firmly, and trust it in life and in death.

Perhaps it will be asked whether this teaching had any effect upon the world of Vergil's day. Did it become more gentle and learn any greater respect for human affection? Did it become more reasonable, and begin to realise the folly of nationalist passion? The answer to these questions is clear. On the political side, everything that was best in the policy of the Roman emperors, in Augustus, in Tiberius and his successors, and still more in those great benefactors of mankind, the Flavian and Antonine rulers of the second century, was governed by the thought, the insistent teaching of Cicero and Vergil, that the good of humanity and not the wealth of Rome must be the centre of the statesman's ideal. Under Trajan and Hadrian this conception spread its beneficent light from one end of the world to the other, and continued to be the noblest element in the thought of the Empire so long as that Empire endured. On the other hand, on the spiritual side, who can deny that the influence of Vergil so deeply graven in the thought of all the great teachers of the first six Christian centuries, so warmly and frankly invoked as an ally of Christianity in

the ages in which it first won its way; who can doubt
that Vergil's insistence on human affection was an influence of unmeasured power in opening the way for the
only religion that has ever striven to make that affection its central strain; the only religion that, rightly or
wrongly, in a cruel world, has ever dared to believe and
to proclaim the faith that God is Love?

CHAPTER VI

THE ROAD TO CHRISTMAS

IF, in the full sense of the words, we were to go into
the early history of the festival of Christmas, it would
take us very far back into the beginnings of society
and civilisation. This may perhaps seem surprising; yet
if one thinks for a minute, one realises that the 25th of
December is not mentioned anywhere in the New Testament. Still, without that, I expect that most of us have
supposed, since Christmas Day is mentioned in the Prayer
Book anyhow—though even the Prayer Book is cautious
—"as at this time" (i.e. 'about this time') not "on that
day"—that the date of Christ's birth was somewhere or
other recorded. The fact is that it is not.

So there are two different stories which might be told
under my title. The first would show how people came
to have a festival at all in the darkest days of winter; the
second would tell us how and when Christians came to
believe that their Lord was born on earth just at that
time. About the first I must only say here that students
of human customs have found in many tribes in the
temperate zones a desire to celebrate with rejoicings
what astronomers call the Solstice; that is, the point in
the year at which the days leave off getting shorter;
when the sun seems to want to be kind to us again.
Of course, to people who enjoy the comforts with which
we make winter tolerable nowadays the Solstice means
very little. But to primitive man in the forests or the

plains, who felt acutely every change of weather, and who found it hard to conquer the darkness of the long winter night, this change in the behaviour of the sun was very welcome indeed; and a thing so important that he connected it in his thought and in his customs with the great unseen Powers that mysteriously ordered his fortunes, that is, he celebrated it in a religious way.

Having seen thus much, we must take a long jump over countless centuries and drop into some Roman town, say in the days of Trajan, about A.D. 100. Let us see in what shape this primitive custom had been developed among the Romans. How did they celebrate what they called the Birthday of the Sun? The days from December 17th to December 20th were a legal holiday called the Saturnalia. The Senate, the Law Courts, the Banks were all closed, and the Schools too; and most people extended the holiday for three days more. During this time, ordinary life was by common consent turned topsy-turvy; people gave up serious occupations, and when they were not feasting at one another's houses, they roamed about the streets calling to one another "Io Saturnalia" just as we say "Merry Christmas". The most dignified persons might be seen wearing a fool's cap—the pilleus—a tall, red, conical hat generally worn only by slaves who had received their freedom. You were allowed to gamble openly anywhere in the streets and no policeman would give you a ducking in one of the public pools, as he would have done if you did this on any other days of the year. At home at meals, at all events at one meal on the chief day, a master waited on his slaves, and slaves were allowed to talk to their

master as if they were his equals. In an amusing poem[1]
in which Horace, after his manner, gently admonishes
his friends and readers by making fun of his own faults,
he puts the criticism of these faults into the mouth of
one of his slaves at the Saturnalia. You were expected
at this festival to make some present to all your friends;
a humble present if you were a poor man, but a hand-
some one if you were wealthy. The most usual kind of
gift, if nothing more occurred to you, was either a little
doll generally made of terracotta, or, for poor people,
of dough baked hard; or else little wax candles which
were burnt when you celebrated the feast at home, like
our candles on Twelfth-night cakes or on a Christmas
tree; what would a Christmas tree be without candles?
At the feast you elected a mock-king, and he directed
all the revels just as our mock-king does, or used to do,
at a Twelfth-night party. Everybody was interested in
the making or giving of presents. We have an amusing
poem of the republican poet Catullus, half a century
earlier than Augustus, who complains of a present which
a friend had sent him 'on the Saturnalia, the best day
of all the year'; it was a dull book, so 'frigid', he calls
it, that it gave him 'a violent cold'!

There is a book of epigrams written by the poet
Martial consisting of over a hundred and twenty little
couplets of verse. I had never pictured to myself clearly
the object of this book, nor what one may guess made
it the most popular (and probably the most lucrative) of
all the poet's publications, before one Christmas Eve
which I spent in the United States. To enliven my soli-
tude I decided to send a greeting home by cable; so I

[1] Sat. 2. 7.

turned into an office of the Western Union Telegraph Company and sat down to write my message. But I was accosted by a bright young person who submitted to me a long programme of greetings ready printed, of varying length and cordiality, any one of which could be sent at less cost than if I had composed it myself. They were intended to save the customer trouble by providing him with appropriate messages to his nearer or more distant relatives and friends. Their merits and comparative cheapness were warmly commended to my notice, and I had some difficulty in securing permission to compose my own greeting.

In the same way these brief couplets of Martial were meant to be put on or with the presents which people sent, and so to add to the gift a pleasant literary flavour, as though the giver had not merely made or bought the gift, but had used his poetic talent to produce a neat epigram to gratify his friend.

Some of the presents were very costly, like elephants' tusks to serve as legs for a sofa or for a table of cedar-wood, or a dwarf slave. Others were more modest—a chained falcon; books like volumes of Cicero, or Vergil, or a Summary of Livy's History; and all kinds of statues and articles of clothing—caps, comforters, shoes or cloaks, jewels, pottery, knives, musical instruments; for all these and many more Martial writes little labels in verse.

You see at once in how many ways the pagan Saturnalia resembled our Christmas—greetings out of doors and indoors, great hospitality, feasting and games of make-believe, wearing a fool's cap, dolls, candles and all sorts of presents, and greetings in verse.

Now what were the early Christians to do about it?

The festival was linked with some of the pleasantest features of pagan life as well as with a great deal of what was less desirable—drunkenness, for example; you were thought to be a quite unsociable person if you were sober all through the Saturnalia!

Well, we know what the Christians' first instinct was. We have many passages about it in the early Christian writers; for instance, the learned Bishop Clement of Alexandria, writing about A.D. 200, says that only the over-curious[1] can pretend to know the date, as well as the year, of Christ's birth, though he thinks himself that the likeliest date was November 18th in 3 B.C. His pupil, the great theologian Origen,[2] early in the third century several times repeats a remark which he says he took from one of his predecessors,[3] that no just man or Christian saint had ever kept a birthday, his own or anyone else's. It was only evil persons like Pharaoh or Herod whose birthday celebrations were mentioned in the Scriptures. This shows pretty clearly that if he had ever heard of such a festival as Christmas he repudiated it entirely, especially as his discussion in the second passage is connected in a rather curious way with the birth of Christ, so that he could hardly have avoided the mention of the Feast of the Nativity if it had existed. But there seems to be no evidence that he ever had heard of it; it is agreed by historians that there is no mention of the festival before the fourth century A.D., while there

[1] περιεργότερον, *Stromata*, i. c. 21. Migne, Pat. Graec. viii. 885 (Potter, p. 407).

[2] οὐδαμοῦ δίκαιος φαίνεται γενέθλιον ἄγων ἡμέραν, *Selecta in Genes.* (Migne, Pat. Graec. xii. p. 132A) and more fully *Hom. in Levit.* viii. (Migne, Pat. Graec. xii. p. 495A–B); *Commentary on Matth.* c. 14 (Migne, Pat. Graec. xiii. 896A).

[3] The Jesuit editors conjecture that this was Philo.

is a good deal of evidence to show that it was first celebrated in the course of that century.[1] Even in A.D. 400
a passage once attributed to St Augustine[2] (A.D. 355–
426) denounces 'the devilish practice of giving presents
on the birthday of the SUN'. But St Augustine himself[3]
says that Christ chose that day for his birth because it
was that on which the light begins to grow. And con-
versely the Christian poet Prudentius,[4] about the same
date, regards the two festivals as identical—suggesting
that the sun changes his course in order to celebrate our
Lord's birth—an ingenious turn of thought which may
be said at least to prove the poet well worthy of his

[1] For the details of the evidence, e.g. of its first celebration at Rome
in A.D. 354, at Constantinople in 378 and Antioch in 388, I may refer
once for all to the excellent article by Kirsopp Lake in Hastings' *Encyclopaedia of Religion and Ethics*, vol. iii. (1910); especially his quotations
from St Chrysostom and the Codex Theodosii, which show that in
A.D. 389 Christmas was not included in the list of holidays, whereas in
a regulation of A.D. 400 performances in theatres and circuses were
forbidden, not merely on Sundays and at Easter, but at Christmas and
Epiphany. I should add that Lake mainly follows Hermann Usener's
Weihnachtsfest (Part I of his *Religionsgeschichtliche Untersuchungen*, 1889);
though he gives throughout a reasonable consideration to the criticism
of L. Duchesne, *Origines du Culte Chrétien*, ed. 3, 1902, translated
into English under the title *Christian Worship*, 1903. Lake holds
with good reason that the plainest motive of the Christian authorities
for adopting the date of December 25th was to convert the Mithraic
festival of the Sun's birthday into a Christian feast; but he admits that
the festival absorbed practices of the Saturnalia. Students of the ecclesiastical mind may find in his article some curious details of the methods
by which the Christian Fathers found arithmetical and Biblical justifica-
tion for this particular date.

[2] *diabolicas strenas* (Migne, Pat. Lat. xxxix. pp. 2002–2004).

[3] Sermon cxc. Section 1 (Migne, Pat. Lat. xxxviii. p. 1007, cf.
cclxxxix. Sec. 5, Migne, Pat. Lat. xxxviii, p. 1311).

[4] Quid est quod arctum circulum
    Sol iam recurrens deserit?
    Christusne terris nascitur
    Qui lucis auget tramitem?
Hymn vii. Kal. Ianuar. (Migne, Pat. Lat. lix. p. 889).

name. Pope Leo the Great, half a century later, denounces those who honour the date 'less for being the
day of the birth of Christ than because it is the beginning
of a new Solar year'; this he calls a 'pestilential belief'.[1]
The date itself was finally fixed on December 25th, after
a long and sometimes violent controversy, the motives
of which are matters of reasonable conjecture, rather
than of knowledge.

But behind such doubts about details, there stands out
clear one of the most pleasant and significant facts in
history; namely, that in one way or another the pagan
festival of the Saturnalia was transformed into an occasion of Christian rejoicing; and that the Christians preserved the cheerful and harmless aspects of the heathen
custom, leaving behind as much as possible of the rest.

These things are typical of what happened in the centuries in which Christianity was becoming the religion
of the world. The Christians picked out what seemed to
them to be best in the life of paganism. And if you ask
how they came to think that this was a right thing for
them to do—well, there are many answers that are true;
but there is one answer, not always given, yet very clear
and certain; it is that all the early Christians, including
the Emperor Constantine, were thoroughly persuaded,
partly through a curious accident, that the greatest and
most beloved and most familiar of all writers of ancient
Rome, the poet Vergil, had actually foretold the birth
of Christ in one of his shorter poems, and so had as much
right to be venerated by Christians as, say, Isaiah, or
David, or any of the Jewish poets or prophets.

[1] *pestifera persuasio.* Sermons 226, 261, 274 (Migne, Pat. Lat. liv.
pp. 198, 212, 218).

But were the Christians willing to believe this, merely because of an accident through which they connected one of Vergil's poems with Christ? No, there was a deeper and truer reason, which St Augustine loves to acknowledge. It was in the actual character of Vergil's own poetry.

Remember that Vergil was studied by every schoolboy; a boy would carry his *Aeneid* in his satchel to and from school till it was dog's-eared and torn and black; every schoolboy knew all the story of it, and learnt by heart hundreds of its lines. Juvenal tells us that in his time, not long after A.D. 100,

> de conducendo loquitur iam rhetore Thule.
> 'Thule was talking about engaging a professor of rhetoric.'

By Thule no doubt he meant Britain; and part of the training given by the *rhetor*, as we may see in Quintilian, consisted in studying and probably learning by heart a good deal of poetry. So that to any even partly educated Roman a quotation from Vergil sounded much as a quotation from Shakespeare or the New Testament does to us. So that if Vergil foretold the new faith, it was a great argument that the new faith was good.

But, one naturally asks, how came the early Christians to think that Vergil had foretold the coming of their Master? Let us answer the question first by asking another. What did they mean by foretelling a Messiah? Did they not include in the notion some such ideas as this?

That the guilt of mankind had grown to be unendurable, so that the world was pitiably in need of a new start; that the establishment of the Roman Empire was an epoch strangely favourable to a great ethical movement, and intended by Providence to introduce it, and that it was part of the duty of Rome to attempt the task; above all that one special deliverer would be sent by Providence to begin the work.

All these ideas we certainly find in Vergil's poetry; in the *Aeneid*, we find him saying that a deliverer had already been sent. And there are two other ideas not less clear in that great poem—that the work would involve suffering and disappointment; and that its essence lay in a new spirit, a new and more humane ideal.

Now if these were among Vergil's constant thoughts it follows that, in the truest sense of the word, Vergil did 'prophesy' the coming of some great deliverer whose mission was to be like that of what the Jews called a Messiah. Vergil had read the conditions of his time with profound insight, and with not less profound hope declared that some answer would be sent to the world's need.

None of these points can be called in any sense new to students of Vergil. But we must examine the first a little more closely if we wish to realise what kind of a world it was to which Vergil promised a deliverance.

In the last age of the Roman Republic (say from 133 to 31 B.C.) the sufferings caused to the world by what Horace called the 'delirium' of its rulers had reached an unbearable pitch. By 118 B.C. the Roman Empire had spread over the Mediterranean world; and in the century before 31 B.C. Italy had seen twelve separate civil wars, six of them involving many of the provinces; a long series of political murders, beginning with the Gracchi, and ending with Caesar and Cicero; six deliberate, legalised massacres, from the drum-head court-martial, which sentenced to death three thousand supposed followers of Gaius Gracchus, to the second proscription of two thousand citizens dictated by Mark Antony; and the massacre in cold blood of three hundred Roman senators and knights by Octavian at Perusia in 40 B.C. Men still spoke with a shudder of the butchery by Sulla of eight thousand Samnite prisoners[1] in the hearing of the assembled Senate, and the boy Vergil would meet many men who had seen the last act[2] of the struggle with Spartacus and his army of escaped gladiators—six thousand prisoners nailed on crosses along the whole length of the busiest road in Italy, from Rome to Capua, one every fifty yards. And the long record of the oppression of the provinces year by year under fresh governors is hardly less terrible. The chief causes of this chaos were the complete decay of civil control over the military forces of the empire; the concentration of capital in the hands of the governing class at Rome; and the enormous growth of slavery and the depopulation of Italy. These evils were in Vergil's mind when he contrasted the peaceful toil of the farmer with the corrupt, reckless ambitions of political life, in the second book of his *Georgics*. Hardly even Cicero, and certainly no other man of that generation, felt the shame of that corruption as did Vergil. With scorn he points to the paths by which the great men of his age had won the way to power, especially Pompey, Caesar and Crassus, who are clearly depicted in part of that famous passage:

> 'Some fret with labouring oars the treacherous sea,
> Eager to trade in slaughter, breaking through
> The pomp and sentinels of ancient kings.
> This man will storm a town and sack its homes,

[1] App. I. 93. 5. [2] App. I. 120.

To drink from alabaster, sleep in purple.
His rival hoards up gold and broods alone
On buried treasure. That man's dream is set
On power to sway a crowd by eloquence,
And so command the acclaim of high and low
In vast assemblies. Here the victors march
Proud of their brothers' blood upon their hands;
There steal the vanquished, torn from home and children,
To seek new fatherlands and alien skies'.

In the stormer of towns we recognise Caesar, who, as Plutarch records, took eight hundred cities by assault, and fought with three millions of men, of whom one million were slain and one million enslaved.

What was the character of the change that Vergil prophesied? This will explain a point which may have seemed strange. How can you, it may be objected, see in Vergil's writings any anticipation of a spiritual Messiah, such a Deliverer as the Christians claimed to know, when Vergil declares that Augustus is the deliverer he celebrates, that Augustus' work is to bring the great reformation? But this is a misconception. For Augustus, we know, was far from perfect; his early record was full of bloodshed, and not wholly free from treachery. Vergil was not content with the past or present weaknesses of the particular human being called Octavian, even after he had received the title of Augustus; he condemned roundly, in his early and his later poems, the violent deeds linked with his earlier career. What he praises is only the vast service which Augustus was visibly rendering to mankind. In the passage devoted to Augustus in *Aeneid* VI, there is no mention of his triumphs in war; his glory is the recall of the Golden Age of Justice and good government, his journeying in peace through the

Empire, like the traveller Hercules who tamed the wild beasts of the forest, like Liber the god of the vineyard and the winepress who yoked his tigers to the chariot of rejoicing over harvest and vintage.

What, then, was Vergil's new ideal? It was the conception of peace by forgiveness, of conciliation instead of punishment—in a word, the ideal of mercy.[1] In Vergil's great picture-gallery of Roman heroes, nothing is more striking than the faint praise or open censure which he bestows on those who were merely warriors. Of Julius Caesar[2] we have nothing but a lament for his share in the Civil War, and a word of praise for his efforts to make peace.

The fullest embodiment of this conception is the character of Aeneas in the second half of the *Aeneid*. But that would take us too long to examine here.

Let us turn to the Messianic poem itself, the fourth Eclogue. I must beg leave to take for granted the answer now given by the majority of scholars to the fascinating historical problem[3] which it presents. Written towards the end of the year 40 B.C., at a moment when the civil wars seemed to be coming to an end (because of the temporary reconciliation between Octavian and Mark Antony), it heralds the expected birth of an heir to Octavian, in the old-world way—before the child was born. This child proved to be a girl, much to Octavian's disappointment. But to celebrate the approaching birthday Vergil had embodied in a shepherd's prophecy his hopes for a new era, a golden age of peace, in which

---

[1] See p. 94 f.   [2] Aen. vi. 834.
[3] See *Vergil's Messianic Eclogue* (London, 1907) by Mayor, Fowler, and Conway. See further Class. Rev. xlv. (1931), p. 32 (col. b).

regenerate humanity should enjoy every kind of blessing.

Of the lines which follow, which come (with a few changes) from the version of the poem which I attempted in 1907,[1] the characteristic which we have been tracing is plainly the animating spirit.

The likenesses between Vergil's prophecy and the Messianic visions of the Hebrew prophets, especially those attributed to Isaiah,[2] have long ago been pointed out; and it is generally agreed that Vergil must have had, directly or indirectly, some acquaintance with these oriental hopes. Isaiah connects his golden age in the future with the birth of a child, who is to be a king reigning in righteousness, restoring the innocence of the world, bringing peace between all creatures and between men, so that serpents shall not be poisonous and wild beasts shall become fit company for little children. These features appear in Vergil's picture too. One thing which Isaiah's conception of the Messiah's duty includes does not appear in Vergil, namely his 'slaying the wicked'.[3] By the time Vergil's infant has grown to manhood all the world is to be at peace. And no one, I think, has yet pointed out how much there is in the poem which, so far as we can learn at present, is peculiar to Vergil himself. Vergil cannot think of the birth of a child without unconsciously dwelling on the simple human aspects of such an event. He addresses not his nation, or its ruler, but the child itself; twice he calls it 'little', and once 'dear'. The earth is to provide the child with playthings (munuscula). The blossoms that grow around

---

[1] As an introduction to the joint discussion of Eclogue IV just cited.
[2] Chaps. ix and xi.   [3] Isaiah xi. 4.

the baby's cradle will 'caress' its face (*blandos tibi flores*). The same playful tone appears in the picture of other living creatures; for the she-goats are to come home, unsummoned, to bring their milk; the sheep will grow with fleeces of different hues, so that no dye will be needed to make them into pretty garments; the colours for the child's dress, saffron, scarlet or crimson, are to be there already. The mother is real; she has suffered, waiting long; and the father is mentioned too, for he has a share in the joy.

In the richly interwoven texture of the vision many strains appear—the bodings of Etruscan soothsayers; the subtleties of Greek magic; the jollity of Sicilian shepherds; the faith of a Hebrew prophet; the triumph of Roman conquerors; the speculations of Platonic philosophy—all these contribute something. But what is it that makes the warmth and unity and meaning of the poem—64 lines all told? It is the human affection of which a little child is the centre. This it is which in Vergil's dream is to inspire and bless the world. 'A little child shall lead them'—lead the wild creatures of the forest and the mountain, lead the men and women of the new era and save them from the wildness of the old.

> 'Lo, the last age of Cumae's seer has come!
> Again the great millennial aeon dawns.
> Once more the hallowed Maid appears, once more
> Kind Saturn reigns, and from high heaven descends
> The firstborn child of promise. Do but thou,
> Pure Goddess, by whose grace on infant eyes
> Daylight first breaks, smile softly on this babe;
> The age of iron in his time shall cease
> And golden generations fill the world.
>
> .   .   .   .

For thee, fair Child, the lavish Earth shall spread
Thy earliest playthings, trailing ivy-wreaths
And foxgloves red and cups of water-lilies,
And wild acanthus smiling in the sun.
The goats shall come uncalled, weighed down with milk,
Nor lions' roar affright the labouring kine.
Thy very cradle, blossoming for joy,
Shall with soft buds caress thy baby face;
The treacherous snake and deadly herb shall die,
And Syrian spikenard blow on every bank.

At last, when stronger years have made thee man,
The voyager will cease to vex the sea
Nor ships of pinewood longer serve in traffic,
For every fruit shall grow in every land.
The field shall thrive unharrowed, vines unpruned,
And stalwart ploughmen set their oxen free.
Wool shall not learn the dyer's cozening art,
But in the meadow, on the ram's own back,
Nature shall give new colours to the fleece,
Soft blushing glow of crimson, gold of crocus,
And lambs be clothed in scarlet as they feed.
''Run, run, ye spindles! On to this fulfilment
Speed the world's fortune, draw the living thread.''
So heaven's unshaken ordinance declaring
The Sister Fates enthroned together sang.

　　　.　　.　　.　　.　　.

Come then, dear child of gods, Jove's mighty heir,
Begin thy high career; the hour is sounding.
See how it shakes the vaulted firmament,
Earth and the spreading seas and depth of sky!
See, in the dawning of a new creation
The heart of all things living throbs with joy!'

Last of all he addressed directly the child to be, the
child for which the home is waiting. The thought is
coloured, we may be sure, by remembrance of Vergil's
own boyish days when in his own home his mother and
his father were awaiting anxiously his brother's birth.

And so he prays now that the mother's anxiety may be crowned by the birth of a prince who shall be a Great Deliverer like Hercules and win the world's gratitude and worship, and be raised to receive reward in Heaven, to sit at the table of the gods and to wed the goddess of immortal youth.

> 'Come, little child, greet with a smile thy mother!
> Ten weary waiting months her love has known.
> Come, little Child! Whoso is born in sorrow
> Jove ne'er hath bidden join the immortal banquet,
> Nor deathless Hebe deigned to be his bride.'

It was what we call an accident that gave to the author of the fourth Eclogue such authority among Christians that his teaching was studied as almost an integral part of the Christian revelation; but it was not an accident that his teaching was so profound, so pure, so merciful. Understood in the only way possible to the mind of the early centuries, that Eclogue made him a direct prophet, and therefore an interpreter of Christ; and it is not the deepest students of Vergil who have thought him unworthy of such a ministry.

ADDENDUM

P. 16. I owe to Mr Cavalier's kindness the reference further to R. W. Muncey's *History of Consecration of Churches* (Cambridge, 1930), where ch. v treats of the "Alphabet Ceremony", which the author traces as far back as Tirechan's biography (A.D. 670) of St Patrick. It appears (p. 49) to have been unknown in the East but is given in early Pontificals, e.g. that of Dunstan.

TOPICS

Prayer Book, Christmas in the, 122
Priests, Etruscan, 56; Orphic, 32
Prisoners, slain by Etruscans, 66; slaughter of, at Rome, 68
Processions, ecclesiastical and other, 9; at Gubbio, 3, 7 f.; meaning of, 20
Processions, triumphal, origin of, 51
Prophylactic offerings, 13
Proscription, of 43 B.C., 113
Providence, and the Roman Empire, 129; Stoic belief in, 81; in Vergil, 91, 93
Provinces, Roman oppression of, 131; Roman view of, 116
Psalms, Hebrew, 55
Punic Wars, 117
Punishment, after death, 59 ff.

Questions raised by Vergil, 101

Rehtia, dress of, 12; home of, 11; meaning of name, 12; offerings to, classified, 12
Re-incarnation, in Vergil, 47
Re-interpretation of myths, 90
Religion, Greek, 75 ff.
Religion, Italian, character of, 5, 21 f., 24, 76 ff.; Minoan, 19; Orphic, 28 ff.
Republic, fall of Roman, 100, 102, 130 ff.
Revelation, by Apollo, 93

Sacrifice, expiatory, 62 f.; human, 67; for immortality, 62 f.; vicarious, 74
Saints, of the Abruzzi, 24; worship of, 23
Saturitas, as deity, 77
Saturnalia, Christian view of, 126; festivities at, 123 ff., 125; gifts at, 124 f.

Scipio's Dream, 41
Scipios, the family of the, 42
Sermo, as deity, 77
Sex and gender, 22
Sky, division of, 54
Slavery, at Rome, 131
Slaves, torture of, 61
Snakes, at tombs, 90; worn by Furies and the like, 62
Social War, 3
Solstice, the winter, 122, 127
Somnium Scipionis, 41
Soothsayers, see Haruspices
Soul, divine and immortal, 45 f.; migration of, 32, 47; purification of, 41
Spearmen, and others, 6
Spelling, meaning of, 16
Square symbols, 14
State, ancient view of the, 110
Stoicism, 81
Stretcher, for victim, 7 f.
Suauisuauiatio, as deity, 77
Suicide, among the Stoics, 49; condemned by Socrates and Cicero, 44, 49
Sun, Birthday of, 123, 127

Temples, Greek, 75
Theology, constructive, 25
Thrace, 26, 27, 28, 31; Orpheus in, 28, 31
tibicines, 70
Torches, for torture, 60, 62
Torture, in Dante, 65; among Etruscans, 71; infernal and other, 60 ff.
Tread-mill, Orphic, 38
Trinity, doctrine of, 25
Triumphal processions, at Rome, 51, 68
Triumvirs, Vergil's view of the, 131 f.
Trojan War, 80
Trophy, in Vergil, 71

For EU product safety concerns, contact us at Calle de José Abascal, 56–1°,
28003 Madrid, Spain or eugpsr@cambridge.org.

www.ingramcontent.com/pod-product-compliance
Ingram Content Group UK Ltd.
Pitfield, Milton Keynes, MK11 3LW, UK
UKHW010047140625
459647UK00012BB/1665